MANDALAS, CANDLES, AND PRAYER

A Simply Centered Advent

SHARON SEYFARTH GARNER

UPPER
ROOM BOOKS®
NASHVILLE

To Mom.

Thank you for giving birth to my faith
through your courage, love, and
commitment to following Jesus in all that you do.

I love you.

CONTENTS

ACKNOWLEDGMENTS

Many folks select a word (or phrase) in January to serve as an inspiration to them throughout the year. I decided to give it a try this year, and the phrase that God laid on my heart is from Pierre Teilhard de Chardin, SJ: "Trust in the slow work of God." Writing this book was an exercise in trust as I moved slowly through the creative process. Thanks to the grace and encouragement of the broader community of faithful folks, I stayed focused and trusted that God would provide the words I needed in God's own time. The process of writing was a blessing to me, and I pray that this book will bless others as well. I give thanks for all those who have encouraged, supported, and nurtured me as I slowed down and let the Advent candles light my way.

- To my husband, I am a stronger and better person because of your love. Thank you for helping me see the God-spark in myself and for believing that this book would be born.
- To my daughter, Deborah, you are smart, strong, kind, and beautiful. Watching you grow and mature has been an inspiration to me and to my writing.
- To my son, Timothy, the music you composed specifically for *Praying with Mandalas* inspired me as I worked on this book. I am so grateful.
- To my mom, dad, and mother-in-law, thank you for encouraging me, loving me, and inspiring me through your faith.
- To my sister, you inspire me with your love, patience and perseverance. I am a stronger and saner person because of our lifelong friendship.
- To Grace Harms, my graphic designer extraordinaire, you inspire me and never cease to amaze me with your artistic skill and wisdom. I am ever grateful for our collaboration.
- To my team of readers and mandala testers—Nancy Geschke, Marla Loehr, Sunny Seyfarth, Mary Senechal, and Linda McCowen—your careful reading, editing, and commenting were invaluable to me.
- To my spiritual directees, my own spiritual director, and my fellow spiritual directors, our faith-filled conversations are the foundation of my faith and a blessing to me on this journey. I am profoundly grateful to be a part of the ministry of spiritual direction.
- To the Advisory Board of Belly of the Whale Spiritual Direction and Retreat Ministries, you are my dream team. Thank you for the many ways you inspire me to reach higher, go farther, and listen deeper for God's still small voice in my ministry.

- To my faith home at University Circle United Methodist Church, you have given me roots so that I can have wings.
- To St. Barnabas Episcopal Church in Bay Village, thank you for the blessing of your labyrinth, a source of much healing and centering for my spirit.
- To Pentatonix, thank you for the gift of your Christmas music that served as my constant companion while writing this book. Your music inspired me, motivated me, and kept me going through many instances of writer's block and self-doubt.
- To my wise and wonderful editor, Joanna Bradley, and the entire editorial staff of Upper Room Books, thank you for believing in the practice of praying with mandalas and the many creative ways it can be adapted, enhanced, and introduced to an increasingly wide audience. I am profoundly grateful.

A SIMPLY CENTERED ADVENT

Forrest had been going nonstop all day, desperate to finish his projects at work so that he could get to his sister's house for dinner as promised. Speeding out of town, his mind was a blur of year-end deadlines, presents he had yet to purchase, and the almost annoying presence of twinkling holiday lights. The winding, country road ahead of him was pitch black, with not a single star in the sky to light his way.

Forrest was almost to his sister's house when the silence of the country back roads was pierced by a loud pop and subsequent thuds. He swerved, barely missing the guardrail that overlooked a stomach-churning drop, and came to a stop on the opposite side of the road. His heart racing, Forrest briefly felt grateful to be in one piece. But momentary relief quickly turned to irritation when he realized that his tire was shot and that he would need to walk the rest of the way to his sister's house, making him later than he already was. Frustrated, he pulled out his cell phone only to discover that he had forgotten to charge it that afternoon, and the battery was dead.

Forrest knew he had a dark walk ahead of him as he approached his sister's driveway, which wound through the woods. His car's headlights lit the beginning of the driveway, but they wouldn't get him far. If only he had something to light the rest of his path. Forrest searched his glove compartment for a flashlight but found nothing. Fortunately, he remembered his hastily wrapped gift for his sister in the trunk: a lovely hand-dipped candle with a decorative box of matches.

With trembling hands, Forrest ripped open the gift and lit the candle. The wick burned tall and bright in the darkness. Not stopping for a moment to appreciate his safety or the peaceful glow of the candle, Forrest quickly strode toward the driveway. He only made a few long strides before the candle sputtered and went out. "You have got to be kidding me!" he muttered. Then, in the stillness, a quiet yet unmistakable voice rose from within him, saying, *Slow down, and let the candle light your way.*

What? Slow down? I can't slow down! I'm late enough as it is! Without a second thought, Forrest relit the candle and continued to walk swiftly up the driveway. The flame flickered out once more.

Again, in the silence, Forrest heard those quiet, unexpected words: *Slow down, and let the candle light your way.*

Forrest kicked the stones at his feet but relented. *Okay,* he thought. *I get it. I will slow down, but it's just going to make me later than ever!*

Forrest lit the candle a third time, slowed his pace, and walked up the driveway and through the woods. The candle burned bright and steady, illuminating the path before him. Forrest could now appreciate the gentle rustling of the trees as falling snow filled the air. He took a deep breath, no longer rushing and frustrated, and he felt an unexpected sense of peace. The distractions of Forrest's day began to fade into the background. The blessing of the candlelight slowed his pace and opened his eyes to the beauty that surrounded him. Into the night he whispered with gratitude, "Thank you, God, for reminding me to slow down and let the candle light my way."

We too can embrace the blessing of the candlelight by slowing down enough to see the sacred beauty that surrounds us this Advent. If we rush forward too quickly toward Christmas Day, our candles will sputter and go out, leaving us stumbling through the darkness with no sense of direction. However, if we slow down and follow the starlight to Bethlehem, our holidays will be simply centered in hope, love, joy, and peace. By blending these four sacred gifts with contemplative prayer and mandala coloring, we will learn how to slow down and let the candles light our way as we journey toward the manger.

The word *Advent* in Latin means "coming" or "that which is to come." Each week, as we light one more candle of the Advent wreath, we can see more clearly that which is to come: the birth of Emmanuel—"God with us"—the Light of the world. We wait with eager anticipation. We walk alongside Mary and Joseph. We listen for the angel's guidance, telling us not to be afraid. Like the shepherds, we are surprised by the harmonies of the heavenly chorus. And like the magi, we gaze into the starry night, following its light and bearing gifts from afar. We are active participants in the Christmas story. Each candle we light on the Advent wreath serves as a beacon, beckoning us to draw closer to the radiant Light that is to come. This Advent, may we slow down in prayerful anticipation of the Light of the world that is born in our hearts.

> The light shines in the darkness, and the darkness did not overcome it. . . . The true light, which enlightens everyone, was coming into the world.
>
> —John 1:5, 9

Ironically, this spiritual season of slowing down and focusing on faith has gradually been overtaken by an increasing commercialism and materialism that encourage us to speed up and focus on the accumulation of more stuff. We have been sold the false promise that we can show the depth of our love for others based on what we buy for them rather than how we treat them, based on how much money we spend on them rather than how much time we spend with them. Focusing on the light of Jesus during the season of Advent empowers us to reject the pressure to do more and buy more. Instead, we are invited to savor this season of waiting.

Waiting is a gift—especially as we are entrenched in a society of immediate gratification. Why would we wait when we can have what we want now? We want what we want when we want it—and the quicker the better! But Advent offers us an even greater gift than getting what we think we want exactly when we want it. Advent offers us the countercultural gift of delayed gratification. Or, perhaps, the gratification can be in the delay itself. Slowing down and prayerfully waiting gives our hearts the chance to be filled with hope, love, joy, and peace: hope in the assurance of new life to come, love for each person we meet along the way, joy in lingering with others on the journey rather than rushing toward the destination, and peace that passes all understanding as we eagerly anticipate the birth of Emmanuel.

Many of us feel tremendous cultural pressure not to slow down and instead to race through our days at breakneck speed—after all, we don't call ourselves "the human race" for nothing. We shoulder the expectation that we must be busy, productive, and constantly available to others as the lines between work, play, and rest are increasingly blurred. Unless we intentionally put on the brakes, the race forward will continue.

I have found the process of coloring to be a practical and enjoyable way to step off the treadmill of life and slow down. In a world of perpetual motion and virtual reality, coloring offers a tangible way to find stillness. When I combine the simple act of coloring with the power of prayer, the spiritual practice of contemplative coloring is born. Contemplative coloring gives us a powerful way to slow down, simplify, savor the season of Advent, and create space for much needed prayerful rest. We may be familiar with these words from Genesis: "On the seventh day God finished the work that he had done, and he rested on the seventh day from all the work that he had done" (2:2), but how often do we consider what they mean for our lives? If God needs at least one out of every seven days to rest, why would we need any less? Because of our humanity, we may need even more.

Jesus also understands the importance of designating time for prayerful rest, both for himself and for others. Regularly, after a busy day of healing the sick, feeding the hungry, and teaching his disciples, Jesus takes time pray. Additionally, he encourages others to do likewise. When he visits his friends Mary and Martha, he commends Mary for taking time to sit and rest at his feet. Martha, on the other hand, is worried and distracted, choosing to stay busy rather than take even a moment to be still with Jesus. It is worth noting that Martha's tasks are not unimportant. Showing hospitality to a visitor and caring for her family's needs are certainly vital tasks

> In the morning, while it was still very dark, [Jesus] got up and went out to a deserted place, and there he prayed.
> —Mark 1:35
> (See also Luke 5:16; Matthew 14:23.)

that require attention—but only after first choosing "the better part" (John 10:42) through rest and renewal at Jesus' feet.

How do we choose "the better part" when we have so many important tasks to be done? In this era of 24/7 work and availability, we feel that we can't step away for a moment from our inboxes, to-do lists, and smartphones. We fear that we will miss something important or not be able to respond immediately—as has become the unhealthy expectation. Simplifying our lives and slowing down are countercultural. We have much to do, and we feel as though we don't have enough time to do it all. Yet Jesus encourages us to step away from our distractions, even if only for a short while. Only then can we return to the responsibilities of our lives with a God-centered heart rather than a self-centered heart.

Sometimes only a crisis has the power to get our attention and force us to step back from our busy lives. Coincidentally, while working on the manuscript for this book about the importance of slowing down, I had a health scare of my own that forced me to stop and reevaluate my life. The scare turned out to be much ado about nothing, but when the doctor said I was probably overextended and needed to slow down, I nearly laughed out loud. I wasn't doing a very good job of practicing what I preach! When I pointed out the irony of the situation to my physician, he laughed and said, "We often teach what we most need to learn." Such wise words! The act of slowing down and resting challenges me, and I imagine it challenges others as well.

I have found that I need tangible reminders—especially during the busy Christmas season—to help me slow down and turn away from the distractions that swirl around me. I need ways to engage my hands, my head, and my heart to become fully engaged in my time of prayer. Only then can I recenter my Advent experience in the light of the Christ child. Without a hands-on element incorporated into my time of prayer, I am far more easily distracted. Two tangible prayer practices have proven to be especially helpful with keeping me focused and centered during the season of Advent. Those two practices are praying with mandalas (sacred circular designs) and lighting the candles of the Advent wreath.

In recent years, coloring and praying with mandalas have become the cornerstone of my prayer life. What began as a simple throwback to my childhood love of coloring has become an indispensable way for me to keep the distractions at bay while praying. Contemplative coloring has opened my eyes and my heart to a new way of encountering God. It is tangible, enjoyable, and meaningful. I have rediscovered prayer as something that I love to do rather than something I feel that I should do.

Sacred circular designs especially help me stay centered in God. I tried coloring and praying with a variety of different designs and noticed that certain mandalas seemed to lend themselves more readily to particular methods of prayer. So I met with a graphic designer friend who helped me develop four mandala designs intentionally created to enter more deeply into four specific methods of prayer: *lectio divina*, intercessory prayer, Centering Prayer, and the Ignatian Examen. As I shared these designs with others, I discovered that I was not alone in finding praying with mandalas to be a creative and meaningful way to let go of distractions, stay focused, and spend time with God on purpose. And thus, by the grace of God, my first book, *Praying with Mandalas: A Colorful, Contemplative Practice*, was born, introducing others to this creative way of prayer. Since this may be a new concept for some readers, I've included a quick review of the three basic principles of praying with mandalas. Quite simply—and as my previous book title states—praying with mandalas is a **colorful, contemplative practice.**

- **Praying with mandalas is colorful.** Coloring is a tangible way to pray that engages body, mind, and spirit. In this electronic age, we spend much of our time using technological gadgets. Colored pencils, pens, crayons, and paper bring our attention back to the world around us. Engaging both sides of our brain through coloring helps us stay focused and leave some of the distractions of our day behind—even if only for a few moments. In addition, the designs are intentionally simple, allowing them to be fully colored within a relatively short period of time. Some of the beautiful, complex coloring books that are now available can be so intricate as to become stressful for me to color rather than relaxing and prayerful. Remember also that there is no right or wrong way to color while praying; color inside the lines, outside the lines, on the lines, or even create new lines. Coloring takes us out of our heads and into our hearts through the use of our hands.

- **Praying with mandalas is contemplative.** Contemplative prayer is not reserved for mystics, saints, and monks. A *contemplative* is someone who seeks to create sacred space *(temple)* to be with *(con)* God in stillness. The circular mandala designs are a visual reminder to center ourselves in God and create sacred space to hear God's still small voice amidst the endless noise of the world around us. When we turn inward to seek God's presence in contemplative silence, solitude, and stillness, we are then better able to turn our focus outward and actively care for God's people with compassion, peace, and mercy. Praying with mandalas helps us embrace this life of an *everyday contemplative*—one who intentionally creates sacred space to be still with God every day.

- **Praying with mandalas takes practice.** As with any other activity, prayer takes practice. The more we exercise our "prayer muscles," the stronger they become. For this reason, finding an enjoyable prayer practice is essential. When prayer becomes a dull or cumbersome obligation, we will be less likely to practice it regularly. Because I enjoy contemplative coloring so much, I can more easily embrace a prayer routine. Even the practice of returning to the same mandala design repeatedly has become enjoyable and comforting rather than tedious. My "prayer muscles" have become conditioned so that when I see these familiar mandalas, my heart, mind, and spirit move naturally into prayer. I feel as though I am sitting down with a dear old friend—I don't have to become reacquainted each time I want to enter into meaningful conversation with God. The practice of praying with these few, simple mandala designs offers infinite possibilities for meaningful prayer.

Mandalas, Candles, and Prayer builds on these three basic principles of praying with mandalas and expands them with new mandala designs created specifically for use with the Advent wreath. Like a mandala, the Advent wreath is a sacred circular design and, as such, is another tangible way to keep God at our center.

We set aside the liturgical season of Advent, which begins four Sundays before Christmas Day, as a time to prepare ourselves for Jesus' birth. An Advent wreath helps us focus on the coming light of Christ. It traditionally consists of four candles around the edge of a wreath with a Christ candle at the center. Evergreen branches are often used in Advent wreaths to remind us that even in the darkness of winter, new life surrounds us. In fact, the evergreen holly bush produces its berry in winter—a powerful symbol of how we can bear fruit even in the darkest times.

The colors we use for the candles of the Advent wreath are also significant. Historically, the color of the candles for the first, second, and fourth Sundays of Advent is purple, which reminds us of Christ's royalty (purple has historically been the most expensive dye to produce). In recent years, however, some churches have begun to use dark blue (the color of the night sky just before dawn) rather than purple as a way to differentiate between the liturgical seasons of Lent (usually associated with purple) and Advent. The third Sunday of Advent is set apart with a pink candle to remind us of the presence of joy in the process of waiting. Finally, the Christ candle (typically white) is placed in the center of the wreath to be lit on Christmas Eve or Christmas morning.

> The candles of the Advent wreath, which represent hope, love, joy, and peace, help us to stay centered in God as we anticipate the coming of the Light of the world.

When we light the candles of the Advent wreath, we remember and anticipate the arrival of the Light of the world—a light that will shine so brightly that the darkness will not overcome it. (See John 1:5.) The candles of the Advent wreath provide visual touchstones that bring us back to our spiritual center amidst the hustle and bustle of the season. The four candles of the Advent wreath (hope, love, joy, and peace) each represent a sacred gift that helps us to stay centered in God as we slow down and let the candles of the Advent wreath light our way to Christmas Day.

Christmas Day represents more than the story of a baby born in a humble manger thousands of years ago. The miracle of Christmas is that God continues to be reborn every day in the manger of our hearts. We give birth to hope amidst despair, love amidst fear, joy amidst worry, and peace amidst doubt. Through Jesus, God embraces the fullness of humanity and walks with us. These sacred gifts of hope, love, joy, and peace will light our path as we journey toward Bethlehem.

Each of the following chapters will focus on one of these gifts as seen through the lens of Advent. Although each gift is unique, they also dance together in beautiful ways that sometimes make it difficult to distinguish one from another. Throughout the weeks to come, know that when we focus on hope, we may experience moments of deep love as well. When we focus on peace, we may be opening our hearts to new places of joy that were previously unknown to us. When we center ourselves in the light of Christ, we begin to see how the gifts of hope, love, joy, and peace are interwoven in our lives in mysterious and inspiring ways.

Additionally, I have paired each of these gifts with a particular method of contemplative prayer that I believe will draw us more fully into a meaningful experience of Advent. We will experience hope more deeply through the Ignatian Examen, love through intercessory prayer, joy through *lectio divina,* and peace through Centering Prayer. The chapters that follow offer simple resources to help us stay focused on the Light of the world through these methods of contemplative prayer. Each chapter contains the following elements:

- short vignettes and reflections on the weekly theme,
- suggestions for use with a specific method of contemplative prayer,
- a candle-lighting liturgy for use with the Advent wreath,
- questions for contemplation and conversation,
- seven copies of the prayer mandala created for that week's theme.

Each chapter is intentionally brief so that we can focus our attention on coloring and the prayerful connection with God that emerges from praying with the mandalas. By keeping each chapter simple, I hope we will have more time to rest at the feet of Jesus and savor our time spent with God.

The prayer mandalas have been carefully designed to help us enter more deeply into the four weekly themes and methods of contemplative prayer. Each design is unique; however, one element shines through them all. They all include patterns found in rose stained-glass windows. A rose window is an example of a sacred circular design that has told the stories of our Christian faith and drawn people closer to God for centuries. When light shines through stained-glass windows, different colors and hues are revealed, depending on the time of day or the season. In much the same way, Christ's light reveals different layers of beauty within us, depending on the season of our lives. Lighting the candles of the Advent wreath creates a sacred opportunity for the light of Christ to shine through the events of our lives, illuminating the beauty within us and around us in new ways.

The practice of lighting Advent candles combined with the practice of contemplative coloring creates sacred space where we can be still with God. Coloring as a spiritual practice may be new to some, but I invite readers to open their hearts and give it a try. It is never too late to try something new. In fact, my mother began painting at seventy-two years old and has blossomed into a tremendous artist. The time she can devote to her painting waxes and wanes, depending on her level of interest and time available. Even so, all her paintings are sacred works of art, created out of a connection with God that lies deep within her heart and soul. It is the same with coloring mandalas. The colorful mandalas that we prayerfully create while spending time with God are sacred works of art. I hope that praying with mandalas may be just one practice in our prayer toolbox that will help us draw closer to God.

As we enter this season of Advent, may we move forward with an open heart, allowing the God's presence to reach us in unexpected, delightful, and possibly challenging ways. May we be willing to step out of our comfort zones, expand our hearts, and open our eyes to a fresh, new encounter with God amidst the familiar traditions of Advent and Christmas. May the practice of coloring mandalas, lighting candles, and praying regularly offer us the strength to resist the cultural chaos of the season so we can stay simply centered in God this Advent. The blessing of the candlelight will help us slow our pace and open our eyes to see the beauty that surrounds us. Then, like Forrest, we will whisper with gratitude into the silent night, "Thank you, God, for reminding me to slow down and let the candle light my way."

TEN TIPS FOR CONTEMPLATIVE COLORING

1. Everyone is an artist.
You are wonderfully made in the image of God, your Creator. Therefore, you have creative gifts embedded within you. Trust that you are a work of art created by God. Whatever you create will be a work of art as well.

2. Set aside time.
Designate time in your day to be with God on purpose. You may choose to mark your prayer time as an appointment with God on your calendar. Determine what works best for you within the flow of your daily life. Allow yourself to let go of your distractions and sit at the feet of Jesus to color and pray on a regular basis.

3. Set aside sacred space.
You may find setting aside time for God easier if you set aside a space dedicated solely to prayer. Focusing on prayer can be difficult if you sit at your desk, staring at a pile of bills. Set aside a special space and gather items you will need for prayer—a Bible, mandalas, colored pencils, a candle, a journal, and so on. Create a space that is comfortable and inviting so that you will long to spend time there in prayer.

4. Lines are optional.
In contemplative coloring, the lines are merely suggestions. Color within them, color on them, draw new lines, and draw beyond the lines. Anything goes!

5. No color is off-limits.
Pick the colors that attract you or that hold meaning for you. Don't overthink color selection so that it becomes a distraction of its own. Whatever colors you choose will be the right ones.

6. Leave blank space.
There is no need to "finish" coloring a mandala. You can leave blank space that you return to later. The blank spaces may even become integral parts of your prayerful creation.

7. Use colored pencils or crayons with this book.

Colored pencils are a favorite of mine when it comes to coloring. If you are an experienced artist, you may prefer professional quality pencils. However, I have not found that expensive pencils work any better than inexpensive ones. I do see value in spending a little extra to get a wide variety of colors and shades. I also enjoy using soy-based crayons. Not only are they better for the environment but you can use your finger to blend the colors to create some nice effects.

8. Spin the mandala.

Remember that you can spin this book any direction you wish so that you can color comfortably whether you are left-handed or right-handed.

9. Breathe.

This may seem self-evident. However, in moments of great focus, you may find yourself holding your breath in concentration. Relax and breathe deeply while you color and pray.

10. The sky's the limit!

Perhaps one of the most important things to remember is that there is no right way to color. Release any preconceived notion you have about the process. Embrace your inner child, and follow where the Spirit leads. Your focus is the journey, not the destination.

HOW TO USE THIS BOOK

I pray that *Mandalas, Candles, and Prayer*, which can be used as a personal practice, a family devotion, or a small-group study, will be a source of joy and spiritual renewal during Advent. Whether used individually or with others, *Mandalas, Candles, and Prayer* will be more meaningful if used in conjunction with an Advent wreath. In order to facilitate this, each chapter includes a candle-lighting liturgy to be used during the weekly lighting of the Advent candles. An Advent wreath needn't be elaborate—you only need four simple candles arranged in a circle (preferably three purple or blue and one pink) with one white candle in the center. You can use real candles or battery-powered candles. You can get fancy and add holly or greenery around the outer circle, but an actual garland or wreath is not necessary. The candles of the wreath are traditionally lit on the four Sundays of Advent. However, as you color and pray throughout the rest of the days of the week, I suggest you pick a separate candle to light while you color. The gentle glow of candlelight each day will serve as a reminder of the light of the Christ child.

This section includes practical tips on when to begin using this book as well as suggestions on how to use this resource as an individual, as a family, or with a small group.

When to Begin *Mandalas, Candles, and Prayer*

You may be asking yourself, *When should I begin the process of coloring and praying through the four weeks of Advent?* This is a trickier question than you might expect. Because Christmas falls on a different day of the week each year, sometimes the fourth week of Advent can get shortchanged. For example, if the fourth Sunday of Advent and Christmas Eve fall on the same day, you won't have time to savor the theme of the fourth week before leaping straight into Christmas the following day. However, if Christmas falls a week later than the fourth Sunday of Advent, you get a full seven days in which to focus on that week's theme.

Because of this change from year to year, I offer two suggestions for when to begin coloring and praying during the four weeks of Advent. Both paths are equally meaningful, so choose whichever option feels most comfortable for you.

1. Begin the Monday prior to the first Sunday of Advent, and enjoy the devotional readings and daily mandala coloring that lead up to the weekly lighting of the candles on the

Advent wreath. The benefit to this approach is that the lighting of the candles becomes a culmination of your reflections on the weekly theme. This method also allows you to enjoy seven full days of each week of Advent, regardless of the day of the week on which Christmas falls.

2. Begin on the first Sunday of Advent and enjoy the devotional readings and daily mandala coloring during the days that follow the weekly lighting of the candles on the Advent wreath. The benefit to this approach is that the lighting of the candles sets the stage for your reflections on the theme for the week to come. In differing years, you will have anywhere from one to seven days to observe the fourth week of Advent, depending on the day of the week Christmas falls.

How to Use as a Personal Devotion

Designate time in your daily routine for coloring and prayer, offering yourself grace if the day's events occasionally interfere. Set aside a space where you can place your Advent wreath (for use on Sunday), a separate candle (for use on the remaining days of the week), your book, a Bible, and coloring supplies. If you cannot designate a space for coloring and prayer, consider putting your items in a basket or box that you can take wherever you plan to pray.

On Sundays, light the corresponding candle(s) of the Advent wreath, and use the candle-lighting liturgy included with each chapter. For example, on the first Sunday of Advent, you will only light the first candle. On the second Sunday of Advent, you will light both the first and second candle. On the third Sunday of Advent, you will light the first, second, and third (pink) candle and so on until you light all four candles, including the Christ candle on Christmas Day. While coloring and praying during the remaining days of the week, I suggest you light a different candle (not from the Advent wreath) as a reminder of God's light in your daily life. After prayerfully coloring a mandala, consider writing a few words of reflection either in a separate journal or on the page with the mandala as a way of remembering the intentions of your heart in that moment.

Breathe deeply. Relax. There is no right way or wrong way to color and pray. When you spend time with God, God delights in your company. Enjoy!

How to Use as a Family Devotion

This book offers a blend of coloring and prayer that allows families to share in devotional time together throughout the season of Advent. All ages can participate fully, making this practice an intergenerational bridge that is both meaningful and fun.

- Place the Advent wreath in a central location where all family members can see it throughout the day as a visible reminder of the Advent season.

- Set aside particular colored pencils or crayons that are only used for praying with mandalas. Family members (children, youth, adults, and older adults alike) will eagerly look forward to prayer time as an opportunity to use these special coloring instruments.
- Designate a weekly time for your family to gather together for prayer and coloring. Ideally, your family would gather on Sunday for the lighting of the Advent candle(s). You may also choose to meet on a weekday to keep the focus on God's light throughout the week.
- On Sundays, read the candle-lighting liturgy together, alternating who will lead the prayers, scripture, and song.
- Determine what length of time is best for silent coloring, depending on the ages and attention spans of your family members. Set a timer for the determined amount of time so that everyone can enjoy coloring without needing a timekeeper.
- Begin and end the time of silence with words from the liturgy.
- As time allows, continue coloring and talking together about your time of prayer. You can use the questions included at the end of the liturgy or simply invite your family members to share what they were thinking as they colored and prayed.
- End your family devotional time with the closing prayer (read by an individual or in unison).

How to Use with a Small Group (Advent Coloring Circle)

Using *Mandalas, Candles, and Prayer* with a small group requires very little advanced preparation but still provides a meaningful opportunity to spend time in community during Advent.

To the Host

- In advance, determine a time and location for your Advent Coloring Circle to gather (your home, church, coffee shop, library, or other appropriate venue). You may choose to meet weekly or less frequently during the season of Advent, depending on what schedule will keep things simple and bring the most joy. Invite folks you think will be interested, and make arrangements to order books for everyone or ask each person to purchase his or her own book individually.
- On the day of the Advent Coloring Circle, simply clear space at a table, and place an Advent wreath at the center. You can put on a pot of coffee or offer snacks, but food is not necessary. If you want to play quiet instrumental music while you color, set up a playlist or a stereo ahead of time.
- When people begin to arrive, simply relax and enjoy. Follow the agenda below that is based on the weekly candle-lighting liturgy included in each chapter. You can read the prayers and scriptures in unison or take turns doing the readings.

- Advent Coloring Circle Agenda (1 hour)
  - Gathering and greeting (15 minutes)
  - Prayer of invitation, candle-lighting, scripture, and song (5 minutes)
  - Silent coloring and prayer (20 minutes)
  - Questions for conversation and contemplation (15 minutes)
  - Closing prayer (5 minutes)

To the Participants

- In advance, obtain a copy of *Mandalas, Candles, and Prayer* (either from your host or on your own), and gather whatever coloring supplies you desire (crayons, colored pencils, pens, and so on).
- Create a plan for daily contemplative coloring throughout the season of Advent as you are able. Practice contemplative coloring regularly when possible, but offer yourself grace when plans change. This book's practices seek to be a joyful addition to your Advent, not just another item on your to-do list.
- For the Advent Coloring Circle, bring your book and coloring supplies. Then, just show up, relax, and enjoy.

CENTERED IN HOPE

Mary, Joseph, animals, heavenly angels, common shepherds, and wise magi from afar—what a motley crew that comes together to honor the newborn baby in a manger in Bethlehem. Nativities from around the world recreate this earthly yet sacred scene in many diverse ways. Even in their differences, they all proclaim the common message that Jesus Christ—Light of the world, Prince of Peace, Emmanuel—is born!

I carry a special fondness for nativity scenes and over the years have gathered quite a collection, including a hand-carved wooden set from West Africa, a Native American scene in a tepee, a corn husk Holy Family, a chiseled olive wood set from the Holy Land, hand-painted figurines from Guatemala (including three women, bearing practical gifts such as tortillas, blankets, and water), a VeggieTales set (with a sweet pea as baby Jesus), and a beautifully crafted porcelain crèche that my husband and I received as a wedding gift. Among all my nativity scenes, a set that I bought last year in Liberia is perhaps the most striking of all: a bullet nativity. All the nativity figures—the animals, the angels, the magi, Mary, Joseph, and even baby Jesus—are fashioned from empty bullet shells.

When the tragic Liberian civil war ended in 2003, the countryside was littered with empty and decaying AK-47 shells. Rather than leave these bullet casings scattered about, Liberian artisan Benjamin Soma gathers and transforms these weapons of war into symbols of hope. He takes the crusted, decaying bullet casings, polishes them, flattens them, and forms them into all sorts of small figurines—crosses, African village scenes, elephants, and even nativity sets. He takes modern day swords and turns them into plowshares. What a powerful way to show that through the Christ child, fear and death no longer have the final word. Out of death, new life; out of war, peace; out of despair, hope.

We focus on *hope* as we light the first candle of the Advent wreath. We pray that the radiance from the candle will enlighten the eyes of our hearts so that we will know the hope to which we have been called. (See Ephesians 1:18.) We pray that even in times of deepest darkness, we will have eyes to see how to turn swords into plowshares. Hope is our belief that God can bring beauty amidst brokenness—like a kaleidoscope whose stunning patterns become visible when light shines through the broken pieces of glass contained within.

During Advent, we slow down and let the candle of hope light our way forward. We step faithfully into each new moment because we believe in the promise that the Light of the world is coming and the darkness will not overcome it. Emmanuel dwells among us to share both in our moments of light and our moments of darkness. We are never alone. There is nowhere we can go and nothing we can do that will ever separate us from God. No matter how dark, lonely, or distant we may feel, we seek to open the eyes of our hearts and claim the hope to which we are called. Hope is the radiant light of God beaming both upon and within us.

> For I am convinced that neither death, nor life, nor angels, nor rules, nor things present, nor things to come, nor powers, nor height, nor depth, nor anything else in all creation, will be able to separate us from the love of God in Christ Jesus, our Lord.
>
> —Romans 8:38-39

Even so, hope is often misunderstood as frivolous or sentimental. But hope is gritty and real; hope is the tenacious willingness to wait for the light even when we are plunged into darkness. A dear friend of mine experiences intense times of darkness when migraine headaches make seeing the light of hope virtually impossible. In fact, she literally has to shut out all external light in order to endure the pain one moment at a time. During these times of excruciating suffering, she searches for a glimpse of hope in the darkness and whispers the words, "I am afraid. I cannot see you Jesus, but I trust that you are there." This woman of profound faith has confessed to me that seeing hope amidst the struggle of intense physical pain can at times feel beyond her grasp. Sometimes the only hope she can muster is the mere memory of the light. She has seen the light of Jesus and has hope that she will see it again. Hope is her dogged determination to believe that the light is still there even if she cannot see it. Hope stands beside each of us in times of darkness and waits with us for our vision to return.

Advent is one such time of waiting. For now, we may only see dimly, but when we arrive at the manger, we will see God face-to-face. God loves us so much that God sends Jesus to be a beacon of light. God weeps with us when we weep, laughs with us in our joy, aches with us in our loss, celebrates with us when we thrive, and stays awake with us through the sleepless nights. We are never alone. Hope is the promise that the Light of the world will be with us to the end of the age. May we have eyes to see.

> "Remember, I am with you always, to the end of the age."
>
> —Matthew 28:20

One way to slow down and open our eyes to the light of the Christ child is through the spiritual practice of contemplative coloring. Recently, a colleague experienced a particularly overwhelming week, both personally and professionally. Within the span of a few days, a young father in his church died suddenly, and his own mother entered hospice with only a few days left to live. He found it increasingly hard to focus on anything at work, so he headed home, pulled out his copy of *Praying with Mandalas*, and began to color. He said, "I knew that I wanted to be with God, but I had no energy to do anything else but sit and color. The coloring helped me to pray even when everything else seemed to be spinning out of control." When the chaos and heaviness of life made everything a blur, the simple act of coloring helped him to be still and open the eyes of his heart to hope.

Especially during the holiday season, when the bustling crowds and bright lights become a blur of activity, we may not be able to see the gentle light of the manger, beckoning us to draw closer. Amidst the temptations to be distracted by busy-ness, how can we stay focused on Jesus? We must commit ourselves daily—perhaps even moment by moment—to choose hope over despair. We choose to believe the good news that the light of Jesus will shine in the darkness and the darkness will not overcome it. We pray for hope and the ability to keep that hope at the center of our lives. Keeping our eyes open to hope as part of our daily living can be challenging. But it is not a challenge that is unique to our time. A well-known saint from centuries ago struggled similarly and developed a prayer designed to help us stay focused on hope and to help us see God in all things.

Saint Ignatius of Loyola (1491–1556) felt that looking intentionally for God's presence in the everyday events of our ordinary lives would draw us into a deeper relationship with God and offer a clearer vision of hope for our lives. The simple, yet powerful prayer that he developed is called the Ignatian Examen. Although Saint Ignatius is known now for his passionate commitment to spiritual formation, he did not begin with a strong commitment to his own faith. At the age of thirty, his life changed dramatically when a cannonball shattered his leg in battle. He was forced to spend years in recovery with only two books at his disposal: one about the lives of the saints and the other about the life of Jesus. His injury, which he initially had perceived as the tragic end of his life as a royal courtier, created space for his own faith transformation. Over time, he learned to see the light of hope shining amidst the darkness of his brokenness.

As the light of Ignatius's own faith grew brighter, he kept notes about which prayer practices he found to be most meaningful. These notes developed into his *Spiritual Exercises*—a book describing his method of spiritual formation, which was rooted in daily prayer, scripture reading, contemplation, journaling, and regular meetings with a spiritual director. One critical element of his *Spiritual Exercises* that has become particularly meaningful to

> The Examen is a daily "check in" with God.

many is a daily "check in" with God that he called the Examen of Conscience, or the Examen for short. Through the Examen prayer, we review the specific events of our day and prayerfully reflect on where we saw or didn't see God. It is a simple prayer that invites us to open our eyes to God every single day. The Examen keeps us focused on the present rather than dwelling on the "if-onlys" of the past or the "what-ifs" of the future.

Many scholars and theologians have explained the Examen process in different ways, using anywhere from two to five steps. Seeing the Examen as prayer in four movements has been meaningful to me. The Examen includes the following four steps:

1. **Emmanuel — "God with us."** Begin by remembering that God is with you always. There is no time, place, or circumstance of your life where God is not present with you. Bask in the light of God, which shines on, around, and within you.
2. **Gratitude.** Give thanks for the moments today when you felt most connected to God. Review the events of your day, and celebrate the specific moments when you saw God's light most clearly. Express gratitude for these sacred moments, and offer God these simple words: *thank you.*
3. **Growth.** Seek to grow from the moments of your day when you felt least connected to God. Review the events of the day, and prayerfully reflect on the specific moments when you struggled to see God's light amidst the brokenness within or around you. Confess that you do not always live as the person God hopes for you to be. Embrace these moments as opportunities for growth, and offer them to God with these simple but powerful words: *I'm sorry.*
4. **Hope.** Look toward the coming day with hope. Expect to encounter God in the specific events that lay ahead. Envision God's light shining through the broken places and illuminating the sacred beauty in all things. Stay centered in hope, and the eyes of your heart will be enlightened.

Practicing the Examen and looking for God in the ordinary stuff of our everyday lives is much like visiting "The Ledge" on the 103rd floor of the Willis Tower in Chicago. "The Ledge" is a large glass box that extends about four feet from the side of the building. Looking upward and outward through the glass, a person can see the broad sweep of a lovely view in the distance. However, if we are brave enough to step out onto the glass floor and look down, we can see the details of what is happening on the sidewalk right beneath our feet. Similarly, the Examen calls us to divert our attention from the distant view and to focus on that which is right in front of us. Through the Examen, we look closely at the details of our day, which requires courage because sometimes we may not like what we see. The Examen offers us a way to look for God right where we stand — in both the good and the bad — and to realize that God is present with us in it all. Hope empowers us to step out on the glass floor and to look closely for God in every moment of every day.

I deeply admire the way my mom actively seeks God every day. She is a devoted pray-er, and I am delighted to share that she has also become an avid contemplative colorer! Praying with mandalas and colored pencils has become a powerful way for her to keep God's light shining brightly in her life. As she continues to color and pray, she is creating a powerful visual journal. She now has a beautiful collection of prayer mandalas that serves as a beacon of light and hope for her even on the darkest days.

Some days, hope can feel as solid as the earth beneath our feet; at other times, it can feel as elusive as a fading mist. But the more we search intentionally for that hope—through practicing the Examen, contemplative coloring, or any other spiritual practice—the easier it becomes to find. Even something as simple as planting garlic bulbs in the fall can become an exercise in hope. The bulbs rest beneath the earth in the darkness, storing energy and waiting for just the right moment to break through the cold, hard ground and to spring into life. I plant these bulbs in the fading light of fall with the hope that new life will come in the springtime.

Hope is the bulb we plant in the darkness, believing that it will burst forth with new life when the light begins to reemerge. Hope is the sunlight shining through and lifting a dense fog. It is the belief that physical suffering will one day cease, that chaos will eventually fade, that we can conquer our fears by boldly stepping out onto the ledge. Hope is having the audacity to work toward peace even in the face of violence and war. It is the persistent belief that against all odds, God's light shines in the darkness.

As is the case for the Liberian artisan who transforms bullets into nativity sets, hope is daring to believe in the ultimate power of God's healing amidst our deepest human woundedness. We are all wounded—physically, emotionally, and spiritually. However, rather than allowing these wounds to become our focus, we choose to hold hope at the center of our lives.

The beacon of hope shines before us in the first candle of the Advent wreath. Like that motley crew gathered around the manger in Bethlehem, we gather around the manger today full of hope. We do not deny the real pain, worries, and fears of our daily lives but choose to center our attention on God's healing light of hope rather than the darkness of despair. We wait with bated breath for the Light of the world, the Christ child who brings hope to the hopeless, healing to the wounded, release for the prisoner, and recovery of sight to the blind. May coloring the mandala, lighting the first candle of the Advent wreath, and praying the daily Examen help us stay centered in God as we journey boldly onward with hope toward Bethlehem.

TIPS FOR GETTING STARTED WITH THE IGNATIAN EXAMEN

The Examen mandala was designed to help you keep hope at the center of your life. It includes four concentric layers that correspond with the four steps of the daily Examen prayer. Beginning at the center, the rays of the star extend throughout the layers of the mandala as a visual reminder that God's light shines throughout your life. Moving from the center outward, the next layer includes six flower petals, each containing a single flame. The two rose stained-glass windows at University Circle United Methodist Church in Cleveland, Ohio, inspired this layer. The flame in each petal symbolizes the clarity brought into your life by God's light. The third layer of the mandala resembles stained glass, symbolizing the way that God's light shines through the broken pieces of your life and creates something beautiful. The fourth and outer layer is made up of twenty-four flames (one for each hour of the day) that encircle the exterior of the mandala to symbolize the light of hope that shines into tomorrow.

Starting at the center, color your way outward through the layers of the mandala as you pray, using the four steps of the Examen. You may choose to pray the Examen in the evening so as to look back at the day just completed, or you may prefer to pray the Examen in the morning and look back at the previous day.

- **Emmanuel—"God with us."** Color the center circle and rays of the star while remembering the promise of Emmanuel: God is with you always. The rays of the star continue throughout the entire mandala to symbolize God's presence throughout your daily life.
- **Gratitude.** Moving outward from the center, color the next ring of the mandala, which resembles a flower with six petals. Give thanks for the specific moments when you most clearly saw the God's light shining through the events of your day. Reflect on the moments when you felt most connected to God.
- **Growth.** The next layer of the mandala resembles stained glass. Humbly acknowledge the specific places of brokenness in your day when you struggled to recognize or acknowledge God's presence. Pray for growth and the eyes to see God's light shining through your brokenness to create something beautiful.

- **Hope.** The outer ring includes small flames that shine the light of hope into the day to come. Pray with hope that God's light will continue to shine into the events of the day ahead.

When you are finished coloring, you may choose to write your thoughts or reflections in a journal or directly on the mandala page, thus enhancing the visual prayer journal you are creating. Writing just a few words of reflection will help you remember what was on your heart and mind as you colored and prayed.

CANDLE-LIGHTING LITURGY FOR WEEK ONE

Prayer of Invitation

God of hope, as I light this candle, color these mandalas, and practice the Examen prayer, help me to be still and stay centered in you. This Advent, may I see beauty amidst brokenness and hope amidst despair. Your light shines in the darkness, and the darkness will not overcome it. Shine your light on me, in me, and through me. May I have eyes to see. Amen.

Lighting the Advent Wreath

Light the first candle of the Advent wreath.

Scripture Reading

Ephesians 1:18-19

With the eyes of your heart enlightened, you may know what is the hope to which he has called you, what are the riches of his glorious inheritance among the saints, and what is the immeasurable greatness of his power for us who believe, according to the working of his great power.

Music

"I Want to Walk as a Child of the Light" (*United Methodist Hymnal* #206)
(Look up the hymn listed above, and sing or read the first verse aloud.)

Silent Coloring and the Ignatian Examen

Choose a length of time for sacred silence and coloring that is best for you or for your group. Follow the tips for getting started, and use a mandala from the Examen chapter for your contemplative coloring. You may play quiet instrumental music if you desire.

- Begin your time of silence with these words: "God, help me be still and centered in you during this time of contemplative coloring."
- End your time of silence with these words: "Lord, hear my prayer. Amen."

Questions for Contemplation and Conversation

Consider the following questions at any point during the week when you desire additional opportunity for reflection.

- How did you show gratitude for the moments when you were aware of the light of Christ?

- How did you grow from the moments when seeing the light of Christ was challenging?

- How did contemplative coloring bring a greater focus to your time of prayer?

- In what ways do you experience hope?

Closing Prayer

Gracious God, light my path as I journey with Mary and Joseph toward Bethlehem. Open the eyes of my heart, and fill me with an awareness of your presence in all that I do, all that I say, and all that I am. Encircle me with your light. Whisper to me in the silence. Slow me down, and allow the candles of the Advent wreath to light my way. Amen.

First Week of Advent: Centered in Hope

Date: _____   *Location:* _____

*For surely I know the plans I have for you, says the L*ORD*, plans for*
your welfare and not for harm, to give you a future with hope.
—Jeremiah 29:11

First Week of Advent: Centered in Hope

Date: _____   *Location:* _____

*Those who hope in the Lord
will renew their strength.
They will soar on wings like eagles;
they will run and not grow weary,
they will walk and not be faint.*
—Isaiah 40:31, NIV

Date: _____   *Location:* _____

I wait for the Lord, my soul waits,
and in his word I hope.
—Psalm 130:5

First Week of Advent: Centered in Hope

Date: _____   *Location:* _____

There is one body and one Spirit, just as you were called to the one hope of your calling.
—Ephesians 4:4

First Week of Advent: Centered in Hope

Date: _____   *Location:* _____

*But as for me, I watch in hope for the L*ORD*,*
I wait for God my Savior;
my God will hear me.
—Micah 7:7, NIV

First Week of Advent: Centered in Hope

Date: _____   *Location:* _____

We have this hope, a sure and steadfast anchor of the soul.
—Hebrews 6:19

CENTERED IN LOVE

A young boy comes to his wise Cherokee grandfather and confides that he is furious with a friend who has done him wrong. "I'm so angry, Grandfather! I don't know what to do."

"My dear grandson, I too have experienced deep anger and hatred toward those who have done me wrong, even though I know in my heart that we are called to love one another. But I have discovered that holding on to hatred is like poisoning my own soul while doing nothing to my enemy. It is as though there are two wolves inside me. One is full of love and compassion. The other is full of hatred and fear. I struggle mightily every day with the battle going on between these two wolves."

The boy thinks about this for a moment and then asks, "Grandfather, tell me. Which wolf will win?"

Wisely, the grandfather replies, "The one I feed."

—Cherokee legend*

We focus on love as we light the second candle of the Advent wreath, renewing our commitment to love as Jesus loves. We are called to love the Lord our God with all our heart, soul, strength, and mind and to love our neighbors as ourselves. (See Luke 10:27.) Yet we too feel the struggle between the two wolves inside us and long to heed the wise words of the Cherokee grandfather by feeding the wolf of love and compassion that dwells within us.

Love is the essence of who we are. At the manger, we gaze into the eyes of Jesus and see the perfect manifestation of God's love embodied through a miraculous birth thousands of years ago. However, just as miraculous is the awareness that God's love is reborn every single day when we choose to embody the love of God that dwells at the very center of our soul—our God-spark. We are created in God's image, and we are good. We are fully capable of giving love to one another because we first were loved fully by God. The relational threads of love bind us—God, self, and other—together, and we are woven into the beautiful tapestry

---

* Story inspired by a Cherokee legend, which can be found at http://www.firstpeople.us/FP-Html-Legends/TwoWolves-Cherokee.html.

that we call humanity. When we encounter only the back of the tapestry, we see a holy mess! But amidst what may seem like chaos to us, God is weaving a spectacular masterpiece of love.

What does this tapestry of love look like? The apostle Paul describes love as "patient . . . kind; love is not envious or boastful or arrogant or rude. It does not insist on its own way; it is not irritable or resentful; it does not rejoice in wrongdoing, but rejoices in the truth" (1 Cor. 13:4-6). The God-spark within us empowers us to live out this divine love—to be patient rather than envious, kind rather than rude, and joyful rather than irritable. However, sometimes we choose to turn away from the image of God within us and respond not out of our best selves but out of fear, anger, or hatred.

> There is no fear in love, but perfect love casts out fear.
>
> —1 John 4:18

From the very beginning of the nativity story, we are reminded of the importance of casting our fears aside. Perhaps Mary is frightened by the angel who comes to announce her pregnancy, so the angel says, "Do not be afraid" (Luke 1:30). Likewise, perhaps Joseph is frightened by his celestial visitor who arrives in a dream, but he is also told not to fear. (See Matthew 1:20.) Even when the angel approaches the shepherds, the angel's first words are, "Do not be afraid" (Luke 2:10). Like Mary, Joseph, and the shepherds, when we approach the manger, we pray for the strength to cast out fear and to allow the Light of the world to shine into our hearts and ignite our deepest capacity to love.

When Jesus speaks of love and when Paul writes of love, the word used in scripture is the Greek word *agape*. Agape love is considered to be the highest form of selfless love, a profound loving-kindness for another person that transcends any selfish motives and that strives to fully care for the needs of another individual as a fellow child of God. Sometimes we refer to acts of agape love as random acts of kindness—that is, love offered without expecting anything in return.

We can share agape love with others in many ways. Agape can be something tangible like taking a casserole to a friend who is ill or shoveling our neighbor's driveway. It can be sending a card to someone who is struggling or donating our time, talents, or treasures to an organization that helps others in need. Agape love can even be expressed creatively through coloring, throwing pottery, or writing poetry.

My father has been creatively expressing agape love through poetry since I was a young

> A Valentine for Sharon
>
> Love is a pink trombone.
> Love is a risk and a celebration.
> Love is huge Toll House cookie
>   of attractiveness confirmed.
> Love is a burst of glitter.
> Love is suffering unto life.
>
>   Love, Dad
>   (Leonard Seyfarth)
>   2/14/78

girl. As a child, I'm not sure I fully appreciated the depth of love that went into his poems. Recently, however, I came across a Valentine's Day poem that he wrote for me when I was just ten years old. This beautiful poem expresses extraordinary, sacred love using ordinary, playful words like pink trombones, chocolate chip cookies, and a burst of glitter. As my father poignantly observes, love is indeed both a risk and a celebration. We can never be sure what sort of holy mess we will experience in the process of weaving the sacred tapestry of love, but we dare to love just the same.

We also share agape love with others through the gift of intercessory prayer. Intercessory prayer is a divine privilege, an opportunity to be in prayer with and for one another. We connect on a deeper level when we prayerfully share our joys and concerns, laughter and tears, strengths and weaknesses. Through these connections, we learn to understand others better, which in turn empowers us to love others better. Even so, intercessory prayer does present us with challenges. Once we experience a deeper understanding of the longings of others' hearts, we often want to fix—or we want God to fix—whatever struggles they are facing. However, we can rest assured that our job is not to "fix" others. Our job is to accompany others on their journeys and to trust that God's love will find a way in their lives. I may not understand the mystery of how God's Spirit dances and swirls in our midst, but I am confident that it does.

Sometimes, we hear someone's prayer concerns, and we earnestly intend to hold that person in prayer. But in spite of our best intentions, that request gets lost in the shuffle of our chaotic lives. I have discovered that coloring an intercessory prayer mandala for someone keeps his or her prayer requests from falling through the cracks. When I create space for contemplative coloring and intentionally lifting someone in prayer, I feel a powerful connection to that person and a deep sense of gratitude for the time spent honoring him or her. I have prayerfully colored mandalas to honor friends on their birthdays (often sending them a copy of the mandala as a birthday greeting), to walk alongside those who are grieving, to pray for healing, to celebrate joys, and to seek discernment.

I hope that the intercessory prayer mandala design included in this chapter will provide opportunities for us to prayerfully connect with others in meaningful ways—all the while, centered in the love of God that unites us all. This mandala has been carefully designed to focus our prayers on individuals, groups, or even a specific event. More details on the design and how to use the mandala for intercessory prayer are included later in this chapter.

As we grow in our experiences of intercessory prayer, we often become more keenly aware of how meaningful praying for someone close to us can be and how challenging praying for someone we disagree with or dislike can be. Yet our call to love one another is unconditional. Intercessory prayer helps us live out this call by providing a tangible way to step out of our comfort zones and love all God's children—including those who are most difficult to love. Committing to this sort of agape love takes tenacity, perseverance, and a graciousness that can only come from God's presence in our lives. We aren't called necessarily to like every person we meet, but we are called to love every person we meet. We are called to love everyone. Period.

A well-known prophet of Israel offers us a powerful example of how challenging it can be to love all people—neighbor and enemy alike. God calls Jonah to step out of his comfort zone and into the heart of enemy territory: Nineveh. Jonah has absolutely no interest in doing anything to help those nasty Ninevites and chooses instead to hop on a boat headed directly in the opposite direction. A tremendous storm at sea forces Jonah overboard and into the belly of a whale (or large sea creature) where he prays fervently to God and experiences a change of heart. So out of the belly of the whale and off to Nineveh he goes.

Jonah's change of heart, however, is short-lived. When the Ninevites actually heed his message and repent, Jonah complains to God instead of rejoicing. He doesn't want his enemies to receive favor from God. Jonah cries out in anguish that he should never have come to Ninevah in the first place. He knows that God is gracious, merciful, slow to anger, quick to forgive, and "abounding in steadfast love" (Jon. 4:2), but Jonah doesn't want this to be offered to anyone other than his own people.

The phrase "abounding in steadfast love" comes from the Hebrew word *hesed*, which is quite similar to the Greek word *agape*. *Hesed* is an expression of a love that transcends our human limitations and unites us with God. Jonah does not want God to offer *hesed* to his enemies. God's boundless compassion, forgiveness, and love should only apply to Jonah's people—certainly not to the Ninevites who had been incredibly brutal and horribly oppressive to the people of Israel.

> *Hesed*—abounding and steadfast love that transcends our human limitations and unites us with God.

Jonah is stunned when the Ninevites are not who he assumed they would be. His expectations are turned upside down when he finds the Ninevites to be welcoming and open to his message. Nothing has the potential to break down our preconceptions of others quite like becoming personally acquainted. Yet Jonah stubbornly clings to his long-held assumptions about the characteristics of the Ninevites—they are dangerous; they are non-believers; they are his enemies. Jonah simply cannot stand the idea of God's abounding and steadfast love being available to all—truly all—people. In a rage, he storms out of town and claims he would rather be dead than see God's *hesed* shown to the Ninevites.

Like Jonah, we all hold stereotypes that often lead us to suspicion at best and hatred at worst. However, when we encounter positive behaviors that are different than our negative expectations, we struggle to understand. Rather than opening the eyes of our heart to a new perspective, we may respond in anger at having been wrong about our initial assumptions.

How often are we, like Jonah, reluctant to share God's steadfast love—*hesed*—with those we don't like or with those who differ from us? Jonah's story reminds us that God's abounding and steadfast love is present for all people. We are all children of God, created in the image of God and capable of loving as God first loved us. Yet, sometimes the God-spark in others can be buried so deeply that we cannot see it.

All too often we run into these folks at holiday gatherings with family, friends, and coworkers. We may carry past wounds from hurt feelings, unkind words, misunderstandings, or past grievances. In situations like these, how do we have eyes to see the God-spark in everyone we meet—the good, the bad, and the ugly?

Intercessory prayer helps us have eyes to see all people as part of God's diverse, challenging, and lovely human family. The act of *looking* for God's image in everyone we meet is the first step toward *seeing* God's image in everyone we meet. If we look at others with suspicion, already making up our minds to see the worst, then that's what we will find. If we look through a lens of fear, then that's what we will experience. But if we dare to look through a lens of love, it will become the foundation for all our interactions.

To help my children (and myself) see others through the lens of God's love, my family and I would occasionally have what I called "candlelight breakfasts." I would light a candle in the morning before my kids headed to school to remind us to look for the God-spark in ourselves and in each person we meet throughout the day. Especially on dark winter mornings, a candle at the breakfast table provided a warm glow to help us start the day with a positive attitude. As the kids headed out the door, I would say to them, "God's light shines through you. God's light shines through me. God's light shines through everyone we meet. Look for it!"

As a parent, I often sense that what I share with my children goes in one ear and out the other—and perhaps it often does! However, this message of looking for the God-spark in all people must have stuck for my daughter. One year for my birthday, she decorated a Mason jar and filled it with slips of paper. On each piece of paper—all rolled and tied with a red ribbon—she wrote "I love you" in as many different languages as she could find. What a truly lovely gift! She had embraced the idea that all the people of the world know love and express it in their own ways. We just need to look for it.

We will find it easier to love others (family, friend, neighbor, stranger, ally, or enemy) when we actively look for God's image. Contemplative coloring is an active, tangible way to honor God's image in others through prayer. When we slow down and pray for someone else, we empower

> Let mutual love continue. Do not to neglect to show hospitality to strangers, for by doing that some have entertained angels without knowing it. . . . Be content with what you have. . . . So we can say with confidence, "The Lord is my helper; I will not be afraid."
>
> —Hebrews 13:1-2, 5-6

the God-spark in us all to flicker and dance. When I focus my time of prayer on the needs of others, I am living into the agape love that I am called to embrace. I color mandalas for people I like and for people I dislike, for people who are like me and for people who are unlike me. I color for friends, strangers, neighbors, and enemies alike. The blend of contemplative coloring with intercessory prayer draws me closer to God and to others in a powerful way.

Dorotheus of Gaza, a sixth-century monk, suggests that we imagine the world as a circle with God at the center. We human beings are the radii of the circle, like spokes on a wheel coming from the center of the circle. When people who wish to come closer to God walk toward the center of the circle, they come closer to others at the same time as to God.* As with this circle image, intercessory prayer draws us closer to God and to one another at the center of the wheel.

The candles of the Advent wreath also help us to draw closer to one another as we are reminded to look for the God-spark that dwells within us all. The Light of the world is coming, and we must let our God-spark shine and look for the God-spark in others. So as to keep this light alive in our daily lives, we need to slow down and let the candles light the way.

> May we release the pressure to do more and embrace the opportunity to love more.

As we continue through this season of Advent, may we release the pressure to do more and embrace the opportunity to love more. God's love for us is beyond our comprehension. We honor God if we can share even a fraction of that extravagant love with others. May coloring the mandalas, lighting the first two candles of the Advent wreath, and praying for others keep us simply centered in love as we continue our journey to the manger.

---

*Dorotheus of Gaza, *Instructions VI*, found in *Called to Follow: Journeys in John's Gospel* by Martha Ellen Stortz (Eugene, OR: Cascade Books, 2017), 37.

TIPS FOR GETTING STARTED WITH INTERCESSORY PRAYER

The mandala in this chapter was designed to keep love at the center of our attention through the practice of intercessory prayer. It was created with many open hearts that can be filled with names or prayer intentions. At the base of each heart, you will find a shape with three points, which symbolizes the Trinity and is frequently found in rose stained-glass windows. The large outer ring is blank so as to provide space to write additional names or longer prayers as desired. Each mandala page includes an intercessory prayer suggestion based on those who were present at the manger. Feel free to use these suggestions or come up with your own. As always, pray however you feel God is leading you.

- **Individual Intercession.** In the center circle, write the name of an individual who will be the focus of your prayer time. Write the specific prayers you have for that individual in the hearts around the mandala. These may be concerns, joys, celebrations, or struggles. As you color, hold this individual and his or her specific prayer concerns in your heart. Although you may long to fix the places of brokenness and pain that surround that person, remember that only God can heal these wounds. Simply hold this person in your heart, and pray that God's love may find a way.

- **Multiple Intercessions.** To pray for a group of people, write the name of the group in the center circle. Write the names of different individuals within the group in the hearts around the mandala. You may also include more detail about each individual by writing specific prayer intentions in the space around the hearts. Pray for each person as you color his or her section of the mandala. If you are concerned about keeping a person's prayer request confidential, write his or her name or prayer concern lightly and then color over it so that the details can no longer be read.

- **Intercessory Prayer for an Event.** You may also wish to hold in prayer those who have gathered or who will gather for an event. Write the name of the event in the center circle—for example, Thanksgiving, a family gathering, a school reunion, a business meeting, Christmas dinner, and so on. Include specific names or words pertaining to this event inside the hearts. While coloring, hold this event in prayer and trust that God hears your joys, concerns, questions, hopes, sorrows, and celebrations.

CANDLE-LIGHTING LITURGY
FOR WEEK TWO

Prayer of Invitation

God of love, as I light these candles, color these mandalas, and practice intercessory prayer, help me to be still and stay centered in you. May I set aside my fears and assumptions and learn to love as you have called me to love. Give me eyes to see your God-spark in me and in all those I meet. Amen.

Lighting the Advent Wreath

Light the first and second candle of the Advent wreath.

Scripture Reading

1 Corinthians 13:4-8

Love is patient; love is kind; love is not envious or boastful or arrogant or rude. It does not insist on its own way; it is not irritable or resentful; it does not rejoice in wrongdoing, but rejoices in the truth. It bears all things, believes all things, hopes all things, endures all things. Love never ends.

Music

"People, Look East" (*United Methodist Hymnal* #202, verse 3) or "Love Came Down at Christmas" (*United Methodist Hymnal* #242)
(Look up either of the hymns listed above, and sing or read them aloud.)

Silent Coloring and Intercessory Prayer

Choose a length of time for sacred silence and coloring that is best for you or for your group. Follow the tips for getting started, and use a mandala from the intercessory prayer chapter for your contemplative coloring. You may play quiet instrumental music if you desire.

- Begin your time of silence with these words: "God, help me to be still and centered in you during this time of contemplative coloring."
- End your time of silence with these words: "Lord, hear my prayer. Amen."

Questions for Contemplation and Conversation

Consider the following questions at any point during the week when you desire additional opportunity for reflection.

- Who did you choose as the focus of your time of prayer? Why?

- If you followed the prayer suggestions on the mandala pages, what new insights did you gain?

- How will you continue to love others in the days to come?

Closing Prayer

Gracious God, light my path as I journey with Mary and Joseph toward Bethlehem. Open the eyes of my heart, and fill me with an awareness of your presence in all that I do, all that I say, and all that I am. Encircle me with your light. Whisper to me in the silence. Slow me down, and allow the candles of the Advent wreath to light my way. Amen.

Second Week of Advent: Centered in Love

Date: _____ *Location:* _____ *Prayer Focus:* _____

Pray for the shepherds in your life, those who watch over you and tend to your needs.

Second Week of Advent: Centered in Love

Date: _____   *Location:* _____   *Prayer Focus:* _____

Pray for the angels in your life, those who remind you, "Do not be afraid."

Second Week of Advent: Centered in Love

Date: _____   *Location:* _____   *Prayer Focus:* _____

Pray for the magi in your life, those who have come from afar.

Second Week of Advent: Centered in Love

Date: _____   *Location:* _____   *Prayer Focus:* _____

Pray for the innkeepers in your life, those who show hospitality to strangers.

Second Week of Advent: Centered in Love

Date: _____   *Location:* _____   *Prayer Focus:* _____

Pray for the unnamed bystanders, those who come to
bear witness with no need for recognition.

Second Week of Advent: Centered in Love

Date: _____   *Location:* _____   *Prayer Focus:* _____

Pray for the Josephs in your life, those who step out of their comfort zone to show love.

Second Week of Advent: Centered in Love

Date: _____   *Location:* _____   *Prayer Focus:* _____

Pray for the Marys in your life, those who deliver God's love in unexpected places.

CENTERED IN JOY

The three members of the family—father, mother, and son—sat quietly at the dented, scratched, and scuffed kitchen table, lovingly worn from generations of family gatherings. In the small but cozy farmhouse, lights twinkled on the Christmas tree, candles shone in the windows, and a Moravian star hung on the front porch. These symbols of a joyful holiday season surrounded the family members, yet they sat silently and solemnly as they ate together that Christmas Eve. The parents were still a little stunned by the foreclosure notice they had found in their mailbox, and they couldn't imagine life anywhere else but on this land. The father's mind was filled with doubt, disappointment, and confusion. The mother's mind was filled with questions, concerns, and worry.

The six-year-old son, Joshua, however, was filled with Christmas joy. "Hey," he said loudly, drawing his parents' attention away from their thoughts. "At church tonight, are we going to light all the candles?"

"Yes, dear. Tonight is the night for the candles," his mother said lovingly.

"Will Harold be there?" Joshua asked.

This question stumped both parents as they looked at each other perplexed. "Harold? Who's Harold?"

"You know, Harold the angel. The one who sings," he said with a hint of exasperation creeping into his voice.

The parents paused and exchanged confused glances.

"C'mon, you know, Harold," Joshua persisted. "We always sing about him at Christmastime—'Hark the Harold angel sings.'"

As the father and mother looked at their son with his eyes full of innocence and wonder, their heavy hearts found solace in his joy and excitement. For a moment, their worries faded into the background and joy filled the air.

With a gentle laugh and smiling eyes, Joshua's mother said, "Why, yes, Joshua. Thank you for that reminder. I do suppose that Harold will be there tonight. It's always good to be on the lookout for the angels among us."

We light the pink candle on the third Sunday of Advent and remember the message of great joy that was proclaimed by the herald angel on the hillside above Bethlehem: "I am bringing you good news of great joy for all the people: to you is born this day in the city of David a Savior, who is the Messiah, the Lord" (Luke 2:10-11). The term *herald* refers to any messenger, proclaimer, or bearer of news about what is to come. In Luke's Gospel, the herald angel proclaims a message of great joy for all people much in the same way that Joshua's inquiries about Harold, the singing angel, bear a message of joy to his worried parents.

> Rejoice in the Lord always; again I will say, Rejoice.
> —Philippians 4:4

Even amidst the challenges of our world—both at the time of Jesus' birth and now—we have good news and great joy to share. Casting aside the darkness of our worries and fears, we stand in joyful wonder before the manger and turn our eyes toward the face of God. We rejoice in the promise that the Light of the world is coming to shine joy into our troubled hearts

As Christmas Day quickly approaches, we may feel overwhelmed and stressed by the errands and preparations still left undone. Even so, we seek to stay centered in the great joy of the season. Instead of submitting to the flurry of activities that beckons for our attention, we choose to make space for joy by coloring mandalas, lighting candles, and praying. God will delight in our company and fill our hearts with joy.

We embrace joy not as a denial of our struggles but as a celebration that God is with us amidst it all. The herald angel does not say forebodingly, "I bring you good news of great joy, but the baby's life will not be easy. He will be a refugee in a foreign land as a child and will face condemnation and crucifixion as an adult. Well, on second thought, no need to rejoice after all! Too much suffering awaits." Instead, the angel brings good news of great joy with no disclaimers. Divine joy is stronger than our earthly worries. Divine joy recognizes our very real struggles yet chooses to sing praises anyway.

In this season of festivities, gifts, and parties, joy can sometimes feel more like a seasonal cliché than a deeply sacred promise. The word *joy* is cheerfully emblazoned on Christmas cards, wrapping paper, and ornaments. We feel tremendous cultural pressure to appear joyful when, in fact, the holidays can be a time of struggle for many who deal with the realities of loss, loneliness, and deep concern for the future. But divine joy is more than false cheerfulness; it is a celebration of Emmanuel—"God with us." God chooses to walk beside us in the fullness of our human experience—the highs and lows, the laughter and tears, the joys and sorrows.

> Rejoice always, pray without ceasing, give thanks in all circumstances; for this is the will of God in Christ Jesus for you.
> —1 Thessalonians 5:16-18

Amidst it all, we can feel joy because God is with us. We do not give thanks *for* the challenging circumstances of our lives, but rather we rejoice that God is with us *in* those circumstances. Through prayer, we can rejoice in the midst of whatever we face. That is good news indeed! God's will for us in Christ Jesus is that we rejoice always—even when we face sorrow, pain, and worry.

Sorrow and joy are not enemies but partners in the dance of life. When one partner dominates, the imbalance throws us off-center and out of step with life's sacred rhythms. If sorrow becomes the sole focus of our attention—no matter how legitimate our concerns—we lose our balance. On the other hand, if we solely focus on joy without acknowledging the challenges of life, then our joy remains superficial. Praying for the ability to rejoice always and give thanks in all the circumstances of our lives helps us reach a delicate balance.

I experienced a powerful example of this dance between earthly sorrow and divine joy while attending the funeral of a beloved colleague. The time of visitation was filled with tears, warm embraces, and aching hearts. But the service sprang to life with a hand-clapping, God-praising, powerful rendition of "Jesus, You're the Center of My Joy." Amidst the devastation of a life taken too soon, we found genuine joy.

How do we stay centered in divine joy when the temptation is to let the bad news of the world become our focus? We stay focused on the "good news of great joy" of Jesus' birth. We stay focused on God's Word, which is a lamp unto our feet that lights the way through all our days. Scripture—along with the Spirit—remains our constant companion and guide. But how do we read, understand, and experience scripture in a meaningful way?

Lectio divina, a Latin phrase meaning "sacred reading," is a contemplative and prayerful way to stay centered in God's Word and enter more deeply into scripture. By focusing on just a few verses of scripture at a time, we can slow down, savor the words, and seek insight from the Holy Spirit. *Lectio divina* helps us to listen carefully for God's still small voice as revealed to us through scripture.

> *Lectio divina*, Latin for "sacred reading," keeps us centered in God's Word.

Faithful people have been reading and reflecting on scripture using *lectio divina* for centuries. In the Middle Ages, the practice of *lectio divina* became focused on four specific elements: *lectio*, *meditatio*, *oratio*, and *contemplatio*. Over the years, many have referred to these elements using different words that are more understandable to our modern ear. For example, in *Praying with Mandalas*, I referred to the stages of *lectio divina* as read, savor, speak, and listen. For the purpose of this book, I suggest another lens through which to view the prayerful process: read, relish, respond, and rest.

As we work through these elements of *lectio divina*, I recommend reading the scripture aloud numerous times. I discussed the importance of reading scripture aloud with my poet father, who often chooses to read his poems aloud. He said, "Speaking and listening are more fundamental than reading and writing. We learn to understand language verbally before we learn to understand it in written form. So hearing the words takes us to an even more basic level of understanding." I believe the same is true with scripture. When I read scripture aloud, I encounter it more fundamentally than if I simply read it silently. With this in mind, let's consider the four elements of *lectio divina* as a way to experience a fundamental encounter with God through Holy Scripture.

Read. Select a short passage from scripture, and read it aloud slowly. Because you are using *lectio divina* to better understand the good news of great joy, I suggest selecting a passage about joy. As you read the scripture aloud, listen for a single word or phrase that stands out and speaks to your heart. Pay attention to the nudges of the Holy Spirit. This word bubbling up from within you will be the focus for your time of *lectio divina*.

> Let the word of Christ dwell in you richly.
> —Colossians 3:16

Relish. Read the scripture aloud a second time. Just as you would with a good meal, take time to relish the Word of God on your tongue. Savor the words. There is no need to digest or analyze the meaning of the words right away. Simply sit with the word or phrase that the Holy Spirit has laid on your heart, and settle more deeply into the presence of God.

Respond. Read the scripture aloud a third time. Respond to your word or phrase by engaging in conversation with God as you would with a dear friend. Share questions, thoughts, and reflections about what this word or phrase means for you today. Be still, speak honestly, listen carefully, and remain open to receiving God's response. Rare are the moments when insights are crystal clear. God may be speaking through the hint of a new awareness in the back of your mind. Breathe deeply, and listen for God's still small voice.

Rest. Read the scripture aloud a fourth time. Then, rest silently and peacefully in God's gracious presence. Linger in this stage of the process with no other agenda than to be fully present with God. Let silence become the sacred vessel for your time with God.

> Therefore I tell you, do not worry about your life, what you will eat or . . . what you will wear. . . . Look at the birds of the air. . . . Consider the lilies of the field, how they grow; they neither toil nor spin, yet I tell you, even Solomon in all his glory was not clothed like one of these.
> —Matthew 6:25-26, 28-29

These four elements of *lectio divina* are rarely as clear-cut as the orderly list implies. We may feel moved to go from the first to the last element or follow whatever flow seems most natural. The goal is simply to spend time with God and the Word so that we may see more clearly the joy to which we are called during this third week of Advent.

Scripture keeps us centered in God when the stress and worry of the season threaten to throw us off-kilter. When our worries become the center of our attention, we put our lamp under a bushel rather than let it shine. Advent is no time to hide our light but rather a time to see and celebrate the Light of the world. Jesus tells us to let our light shine, to set our worries aside, and to trust that God will provide for us. If God cares for the ravens of the air and the lilies of the field, how much more will God care for us? In fact, God cares for us so much that God's Word became flesh to dwell among us in the form of a vulnerable newborn baby. This child grows into a man who teaches us how to let our light shine rather than hide it under a bushel. The Light of the world shines so brightly that not even the darkness of our deepest worries, distractions, and fears can overcome it. This certainly is good news of great joy!

Even so, I experience rough days when my ability to see the "good" in the good news is severely limited by my own bad attitude, grumpy demeanor, or general feeling of being overwhelmed by life. On days like this, I call to mind a *joy anchor* to help me regain perspective. A *joy anchor* is a memory, person, or event from our lives that has brought us divine joy. Regardless of how heavy our lives may feel at any given moment, I trust that we all have at least one memory, person, or event that exhibited true, deep joy that can become an anchor amidst the storms around us. A *joy anchor* could be a childhood memory, a particularly beautiful sunset, an adventure with friends, a person with a ready smile, a birthday celebration, or even a pet.

One of my favorite *joy anchors* is my dog, Bear. The tremendous joy he displays when I arrive home at the end of the day always makes me smile—no matter how challenging a day it has been. Bear doesn't care if I made a mess of my day or if I had a wonderful day. Bear simply leaps in the air with joyful abandon and welcomes me home. Remembering the joy I find in Bear helps me reclaim the good news of great joy that is the foundation of my faith.

Another tangible *joy anchor* for me is the practice of contemplative coloring. I have discovered that unless a prayer method brings me joy, I am much less likely to follow through and pray regularly. At times in my life, prayer has felt like something I *should* do rather than something I *want* to do. Because coloring brings me joy, prayer is now something that I love to do. I long to create time and space for contemplative coloring during my day and guard my time of prayer so that this opportunity to be still with God does not get pushed to the side.

We would each do well to reclaim the *joy anchors* in our lives that remind us of the light of joy that shines in the darkness. When the seasonal hustle and bustle begins to overwhelm, let's take a moment and consider this question: *What holiday traditions bring me joy?* We can then choose to anchor ourselves in those traditions that bring us joy and let go of those that don't.

For some of us, joy comes in big holiday gatherings; for others, joy comes in a quiet evening alone by the light of the Christmas tree. Some will find joy in hours of baking and others in hours reading favorite Christmas stories. I find great joy in naps by the fireplace, walking my dog in the snow, making *krumkake* (a special Christmas cookie), singing Pentatonix Christmas songs at the top of my lungs, and, of course, coloring. Coloring and praying with mandalas have infused a sense of playfulness and delight into my time of prayer. Especially during the holidays, the joy of coloring keeps me centered in God and focused on the "good" of the good news announced by the herald angels.

> Make a joyful noise to the LORD, all the earth; break forth into joyous song and sing praises.
>
> —Psalm 98:4

May we find a balance between honoring the places of genuine concern in our lives and going forth in joy to proclaim that Jesus Christ is born. May we find a deep and abiding joy in the simple pleasures of the season. May we stay centered in God's Word. May we be on the lookout for the angels among us who bear good news and tidings of great joy. And may coloring the mandalas, lighting the candles of the Advent wreath, and praying with holy scripture help us to stay centered in the gift of divine joy as we draw closer to Bethlehem.

TIPS FOR GETTING STARTED WITH
LECTIO DIVINA

The *lectio divina* mandala was designed to help you keep joy at the center of your attention. The mandala includes four concentric layers of design that correlate with the four elements of the *lectio divina* process. The outer two rings of the circle are intended to provide space for writing words if you desire. As you **Read** the scripture the first time, you may choose to copy the whole verse or just the word(s) you have chosen as the focus of your time of prayer. The outer rings are divided as a stained-glass window might be. You can choose to stay within those lines as you write words and color, or you can ignore those lines altogether and write across them. Moving toward the center of the mandala, the next layer invites you to **Relish** the word(s) that the Holy Spirit has spoken within you. This layer includes the four teardrop designs that symbolize the way we look inward and go deeper. The next layer—**Respond**—invites you to speak with God as you would an old friend and reflect upon your word(s). Use this opportunity to begin an ongoing conversation with God—asking questions and listening for answers. The groupings of three dots in this layer represent an ellipsis, reminding you that your conversation with God is never-ending. In addition, the lily design reminds you to turn your worries over to God and to receive God's grace. Finally, the center star beckons you to **Rest** in God's presence.

Find a quiet place where you won't be distracted, and gather whatever items will help you enter into a spirit of prayer—your Bible, a candle, colored pencils, gentle music. Consider the following three methods for coloring the *lectio divina* mandala. Remember that these techniques are all merely suggestions. Follow wherever the Spirit leads you. Slow down, savor the words of scripture, and seek their meaning for your life.

- **Layers**. The *lectio divina* mandala was intentionally designed to contain four layers that lead from the outer rings toward the center. Working your way inward, color each layer as you move through the four steps of the *lectio divina* process.
  - **Read (*Lectio*)**. Select a brief scripture about joy, and read it aloud. Breathe deeply, and listen for a word or phrase that resonates with you. In the two outer rings, you can add color, write the whole scripture passage, or simply write the word or phrase you have chosen.

- **Relish (*Meditatio*).** Read the scripture aloud a second time. As you move to the second layer toward the center, relish the word or phrase that the Holy Spirit has laid on your heart. You needn't reach any conclusions about the meaning of the word or phrase in this stage. Simply savor the word, perhaps writing it in the mandala, and enjoy the process of coloring.
  - **Respond (*Oratio*).** Read the scripture aloud a third time, and enter into conversation with God. Consider what meaning this scripture has for your life today. Remember to both speak with and listen for God as you respond to the word that has been placed on your heart.
  - **Rest (*Contemplatio*).** Read the scripture aloud a fourth and final time. Color the star at the center of the mandala as you rest silently in God's presence. There is no agenda other than to simply be in God's gracious presence.
- **Quadrants.** The joy mandala was also designed with four distinct quadrants. Color one quadrant at a time as you slowly practice the four elements of *lectio divina*. Write words from the scripture passage on the outer lines or throughout the mandala as you feel so moved.
- **Free-Form.** Identify the word or phrase from your scripture passage that resonates with you, and repeat it frequently while coloring the mandala in whatever way you choose. If you prefer not to follow the more formal process of *lectio divina*, you may enjoy this method of reading the scripture, repeating your chosen word or phrase, and listening for any wisdom or insight that may surface as you color. Afterward, journal about any insights you gained during your time of prayer.

CANDLE-LIGHTING LITURGY FOR WEEK THREE

Prayer of Invitation

God of joy, as I light these candles, color these mandalas, and practice lectio divina, help me to be still and stay centered in you. I rejoice in the good news of great joy. Allow me to set aside my worries and focus on your presence. I give thanks in all circumstances, for you are with me. May I have eyes to see. Praise be to God! Amen.

Lighting the Advent Wreath

Light the first, second, and third (pink) candles of the Advent wreath.

Scripture Reading

1 Thessalonians 5:16-18

Rejoice always, pray without ceasing, give thanks in all circumstances; for this is the will of God in Christ Jesus for you.

Music

"O Come, O Come Emmanuel" (*United Methodist Hymnal* #211)
(Look up the hymn listed above, and sing or read the second verse aloud.)

Silent Coloring and *Lectio Divina*

Choose a length of time for sacred silence and coloring that is best for you or for your group. Follow the tips for getting started, and use a mandala from the *lectio divina* chapter for your contemplative coloring. You may play quiet instrumental music if you desire.

- Begin your time of silence with these words: "God, help me to be still and centered in you during this time of contemplative coloring."
- End your time of silence with these words: "Lord, hear my prayer. Amen."

Questions for Contemplation and Conversation

Consider the following questions at any point during the week when you desire additional opportunity for reflection.

- What scripture did you chose? What word or phrase resonated with you? What might this word or phrase mean for you today?

- How did it feel to enter into conversation with God about scripture?

- In what aspects of your life do you see the good news of great joy? In what aspects of your life is the good news of great joy more difficult to see?

Closing Prayer

Gracious God, light my path as I journey with Mary and Joseph toward Bethlehem. Open the eyes of my heart, and fill me with an awareness of your presence in all that I do, all that I say, and all that I am. Encircle me with your light. Whisper to me in the silence. Slow me down, and allow the candles of the Advent wreath to light my way. Amen.

Third Week of Advent: Centered in Joy

Date: _____   *Location:* _____   *Scripture:* _____

Rejoice always, pray continually, give thanks in all circumstances;
for this is the will of God in Christ Jesus for you.
—1 Thessalonians 5:16-18

Date: _____   *Location:* _____   *Scripture:* _____

Rejoice in the Lord always; again I will say, Rejoice.
—Philippians 4:4

Date: _____   *Location:* _____   *Scripture:* _____

Let the heavens be glad, and let the earth rejoice;
let the sea roar, and all that fills it;
let the field exult, and everything in it.
Then shall all the trees of the forest sing for joy
*before the L*ORD*.*
—Psalm 96:11-13

Third Week of Advent: Centered in Joy

Date: _____ *Location:* _____ *Scripture:* _____

I have said these things to you so that my joy may be in
you, and that your joy may be complete.
—John 15:11

Date: _____ *Location:* _____ *Scripture:* _____

Make a joyful noise to the LORD, all the earth;
break forth into joyous song and sing praises.
—Psalm 98:4

Date: _____ *Location:* _____ *Scripture:* _____

Rejoice with those who rejoice, weep with those who
weep. Live in harmony with one another.
—Romans 12:15-16

Third Week of Advent: Centered in Joy

Date: _____ *Location:* _____ *Scripture:* _____

For everything there is a season, and a time for every matter under heaven. . . .
a time to weep, and a time to laugh;
a time to mourn, and a time to dance.
—Ecclesiastes 3:1, 4

CENTERED IN PEACE

Eager crowds gather by the seaside to be near Jesus and hear his words. Because of the crowds of people, Jesus goes out in a boat just offshore so that he can speak to the crowds and be heard by all. He teaches with parables about sowing seeds in good soil, shining God's light rather than hiding it under a bushel, and nurturing faith the size of a mustard seed.

At the end of a long day of preaching and teaching, Jesus is exhausted. He suggests to his disciples that they leave the crowds behind for a while and take their boat over to the other side so that he can have a few moments of peace and quiet. Longing for rest, Jesus goes to the stern of the boat, lies down on a cushion, and falls sound asleep.

Meanwhile, a windstorm comes on the sea, and the boat is overwhelmed by waves. Full of fear, the disciples wake Jesus and say, "Don't you care that our ship is going down in this storm?"

Jesus gets up and calms the storm with the simple words, "Peace! Be still!" The disciples, previously afraid and losing faith, are filled with great awe.

—Mark 4, AP

We too are filled with awe and gratitude as we light the fourth candle of the Advent wreath and center ourselves in Jesus' peace. For the past three weeks, we have centered ourselves in hope, love, and joy. We have colored mandalas, lit candles, and created sacred space to be still and pray. Now, we are only days away from celebrating Jesus' birth. The Prince of Peace is coming to help us be still and find peace amidst the storms of our lives. Jesus says, "Peace be with you" (John 20:21); "Peace I leave with you" (John 14:27); "In me you may have peace" (John 16:33); "Blessed are the peacemakers" (Matthew 5:9); "Be at peace with one another" (Mark 9:50); and "Peace! Be still!" (Mark 4:39).

From the moment of his birth and throughout his life, Jesus advocates for peace. As a

> For a child has been born for us,
> a son given to us;
> authority rests upon his shoulders;
> and he is named
> Wonderful Counselor, Mighty God,
> Everlasting Father, Prince of Peace.
> —Isaiah 9:6

95

follower of Jesus, we can find peace in his presence even when we, like the disciples, are afraid, overwhelmed, and beginning to lose faith. Jesus never gives up on us. If we only have the faith the size of a mustard seed, the promise of peace on earth and in our hearts will grow. We long to cultivate our mustard-seed faith and boldly face the storms of our lives with the words of Jesus, "Peace! Be still!" But how?

Contemplative coloring and Centering Prayer help us to find peace and stillness even in the midst of our stormy lives by returning our focus to God's presence at our center. We listen for the still small voice of God, whispering insight, love, and peace. We open our hearts to the Holy Spirit and breathe deeply of God's peaceful presence at the core of our very being. Centering Prayer can bring moments of clarity, discernment, and new understandings, but often the gift of Centering Prayer is simply the inner peace that comes from being still with God.

Centering Prayer has been a part of the Christian contemplative tradition for centuries, although in recent years it has been growing in popularity. In many ways, Centering Prayer is one of the easiest prayers to explain but one of the hardest to practice. Through Centering Prayer we seek to do the following:

1. Be still.
2. Center ourselves in God by focusing on a sacred word.
3. Release distractions that throw us off-balance.

Sure, these steps seem straightforward enough, but the difficulty comes in taming our distractions and in learning how to quiet the voices around us so that we can hear God's still small voice at the core of our deepest, truest selves. These distracting voices can be persistent, loud, and hard to ignore, making Centering Prayer quite challenging. God speaks quietly, and distractions shout in our ears. Even so, we can practice tuning into the hush of a whisper, letting the noise of the world fade into the background.

Especially during the holiday season, distractions often become our focus. Demands and expectations tug at our sleeves, seeking attention. Centering Prayer helps us release these distractions and reclaim God's peace. It helps us turn away from cultural pressure to do more and recenter ourselves in the assurance that we are already enough in God's eyes. How then do we get started with this peaceful, centered way of prayer?

> "Be still, and know that I am God!"
> —Psalm 46:10

The first element of Centering Prayer is *being still*. This is far more easily said than done. Being still is a profound challenge in a world that values doing over being. We are a "more" culture. We want to do more, get more, and go more. We embrace the drive-thru, quick-fix, sound-bite, multitasking gurus who sell us the myth that we don't have a moment to spare. We need to be constantly busy and stay productive. Stillness is often misconstrued as wasted time. Amidst this barrage of unrealistic expectations, being still can seem virtually impossible

Our lives are like a snow globe that is constantly shaken and never allowed to be still. When a snow globe is in constant motion, it is hard to see the image at the center for all the snow that is flying about. Only once the snow globe is set down can the snow settle. Then we can see and appreciate the beauty of what is found at the center of the globe.

Similarly, how can we see the image of God at our own center when we flurry about in a frenzy of activity? To find peace, we must intentionally make time and space to set the snow globe of our lives down and let the storm settle. Only then are we able to see the beautiful image of God at the center of who we are. If we lose sight of God at our center, we risk believing that our own ego should be the center of our world. To resist this temptation, we must be still so that we can hear the still small voice of God.

Contemplative coloring helps us to create this space to be still with God. It helps us slow down, set aside our distractions, and focus on prayer, paper, pencils, and the presence of God. The Centering Prayer mandala included in this chapter has been designed to help us enter more deeply into a space of calm and stillness as we color and pray.

The second element of Centering Prayer is choosing a *sacred word* that will help us stay centered in God's presence. The sacred word becomes a bright lantern that lights our way home through the darkness and distractions. This step reminds me of the way my Great-grandfather Bard used to find his way home after a long day of teaching and preaching. Rev. Leonard A. Bard was a Methodist circuit rider in upstate New York in the early 1900s. He traveled between the churches on his circuit in his small buggy pulled by his trusty horse, Tiddlywinks. When Rev. Bard was ready to head home at the end of a long day, he would get into his buggy and simply say, "Home." He would then sit back and rest in the assurance that Tiddlywinks would indeed bring him safely home.

Selecting a sacred word to use during Centering Prayer allows us to sit back and rest in the assurance that our time of prayer will bring us safely home into God's peaceful presence. Some people may choose a sacred word from a meaningful passage of scripture—words such as *peace*, *Emmanuel*, *wineskins*, *Holy Spirit*, *green pastures*, and so on. Others may choose a sacred word that grounds them in God's creation—words such as *sea*, *mountaintop*, *wind*, *eagle*, *roots*, and so on. And still others may choose a word that represents a personally meaningful image for God—words such as *Father*, *Mother*, *shepherd*, *home*, and so on. During this fourth week of Advent, let's choose sacred words that draw us into an experience of deep peace during Centering Prayer.

After creating space to be still with God and selecting a sacred word as our centering focus, we inevitably will experience distractions that threaten to throw us off-balance. Thus, the third element of Centering Prayer is *releasing the distractions* and remembering our sacred word so as to gently return to sacred stillness. Especially during the holiday season, our lives are packed with distractions. For months, stores have been encouraging us to spend, spend, spend on Christmas gifts. Holiday gatherings can end up being more about obligation than true fellowship with others. We long to create meaningful holiday memories with our families and friends, even if it means losing sleep and fussing unnecessarily over details in our effort to create the perfect gift, event, or tradition.

My husband and children still affectionately remind me of "The Year of the Crooked Christmas Tree"—a time when I almost succumbed to the futile quest for the "perfect" holiday celebration. That particular year, when my son was quite young, he was wrapped up in his typically exuberant play and crashed into the Christmas tree, knocking it to the ground. I picked it up and tried to set it back in its stand, only to discover that the base had broken in the fall. As I leaned the crooked tree against the wall and swept up the broken ornaments, I struggled with feelings of sadness and disappointment. Our "perfectly" beautiful tree was now all wrong.

Over the following days, however, I slowly began to regain perspective. I would have welcomed the practice of contemplative coloring had I known about it back then. As the crooked Christmas tree became an unanticipated part of our holiday décor, I grew surprisingly fond of its quirky presence. It reminded me that the desire to create the perfect Christmas had become a distraction. Christmas isn't about the perfect tree or the perfect gift or the perfect gathering. Christmas is about bringing our imperfections to the manger and trusting that the peace that passes all understanding can be born into our lives. Centering Prayer and contemplative coloring help us let go of this myth of perfection and return our focus to the Prince of Peace.

When I begin to feel frazzled and overwhelmed by the demands of the season, I try to take the counterintuitive step of allowing more time for prayer and coloring rather than less. Although this is not always possible, when I have managed to do so, I have been able to see God more clearly and feel God's peace surrounding me. Through Centering Prayer, I am able to find stillness, focusing on God and using my sacred word to release the distractions as Christmas Day draws near.

During this fourth week of Advent, I pray that coloring the peace mandala and embracing the practice of Centering Prayer will provide a tangible way to find peace and stillness amidst the storms that may be swirling around us. During this season of waiting, preparation, activity, and anticipation, may we let go of the myth of perfection and open our hearts to welcome the Prince of Peace into our lives. May coloring the mandalas, lighting four candles of the Advent wreath, and practicing Centering Prayer help us to stay centered in peace as we take these final steps toward Bethlehem.

TIPS FOR GETTING STARTED WITH CENTERING PRAYER

The Centering Prayer mandala was designed to help you keep peace at the center of your attention. It contains a five-petaled rose that is reminiscent of the circular pattern in Martin Luther's seal (another example of a Christian sacred circular design). It also includes elements of the rose stained-glass window in the southern transept of the Chartres Cathedral in France. I intended for this mandala to be a relaxing, restful, and peaceful design to color. Focus on God, and allow your worries and distractions to fade away.

- Before you begin, decide on a length of time for your Centering Prayer. Fifteen to thirty minutes is a comfortable length of time for beginners, but you may wish to start with a shorter amount of time. Experienced practitioners of Centering Prayer may choose to go longer. Set a timer on your watch or phone so that you won't need to check your progress while you are praying. You may also wish to silence your phone or put it in "do not disturb" mode so that you won't be interrupted by calls or texts while you pray.
- Sit comfortably. Breathe deeply. Be still.
- Listen for a sacred word (or phrase) that will become the focus of your time of Centering Prayer. Stay open to the possibility that an unexpected word may land on your heart. God's Spirit moves in surprising ways!
- Settle into the silence, and savor this time spent in God's loving, peaceful presence.
- Color in any way that helps you stay centered.
  - Write your word in the center of the mandala, and color from the inside out.
  - Color from the outside in, and end with the word *Amen* once you reach the center.
- When your thoughts wander—a completely natural response—release the distractions. Be gentle with yourself, and simply refocus on your word. Allow it to guide you back to your center. Even distractions are part of the process.
- Draw your time of prayer to a close when you are ready, using words from a familiar scripture passage or prayer. You may also choose to write a few words of reflection about your experience in a journal or on the mandala page.

CANDLE-LIGHTING LITURGY FOR WEEK FOUR

Prayer of Invitation

God of peace, as I light these candles, color these mandalas, and practice Centering Prayer, help me to be still and stay centered in you. Allow me to let go of the distractions and replace my perfectionism with your peace that passes all understanding. May I have eyes to see your light in my life, beckoning me home to your peace-filled presence. Amen.

Lighting the Advent Wreath

Light all four candles of the Advent wreath.

Scripture Reading

Philippians 4:5-7

Let your gentleness be known to everyone. The Lord is near. Do not worry about anything, but in everything by prayer and supplication with thanksgiving let your requests be made known to God. And the peace of God, which surpasses all understanding, will guard your hearts and your minds in Christ Jesus.

Music

"Blessed Be the God of Israel" (*United Methodist Hymnal* #209)
(Look up the hymn listed above, and sing or read the first verse aloud.)

Silent Coloring and Centering Prayer

Choose a length of time for sacred silence and coloring that is best for you or for your group. Follow the tips for getting started, and use a mandala from the Centering Prayer chapter for your contemplative coloring. You may play quiet instrumental music if you desire.

- Begin your time of silence with these words: "God, help me to be still and centered in you during this time of contemplative coloring."
- End your time of silence with these words: "Lord, hear my prayer. Amen."

Questions for Contemplation and Conversation

Consider the following questions at any point during the week when you desire additional opportunity for reflection.

- What sacred word did you select? Why?

- What were some distractions you faced? How did you release them?

- What might you try next time to help you relax more easily into God's presence and leave the distractions behind?

Closing Prayer

Gracious God, light my path as I journey with Mary and Joseph toward Bethlehem. Open the eyes of my heart, and fill me with an awareness of your presence in all that I do, all that I say, and all that I am. Encircle me with your light. Whisper to me in the silence. Slow me down, and allow the candles of the Advent wreath to light my way. Amen.

Fourth Week of Advent: Centered in Peace

Date: _____ *Location:* _____ *Sacred Word:* _____

*Do not worry about anything, but in everything by prayer and
supplication with thanksgiving let your requests be made known to
God. And the peace of God, which surpasses all understanding,
will guard your hearts and your minds in Christ Jesus.*
—Philippians 4:6-7

Fourth Week of Advent: Centered in Peace

Date: _____ *Location:* _____ *Sacred Word:* _____

For a child has been born for us, a son given to us;
authority rests upon his shoulders;
and he is named Wonderful Counselor, Mighty God,
Everlasting Father, Prince of Peace.
—Isaiah 9:6

Date: _____   *Location:* _____   *Sacred Word:* _____

The Lord bless you and keep you;
the Lord make his face to shine upon you, and be gracious to you;
the Lord lift up his countenance upon you, and give you peace.
—Numbers 6:24-26

Fourth Week of Advent: Centered in Peace

Date: _____   *Location:* _____   *Sacred Word:* _____

Put things in order, listen to my appeal, agree with one another, live in peace;
and the God of love and peace will be with you.
—2 Corinthians 13:11

Fourth Week of Advent: Centered in Peace

Date: _____   *Location:* _____   *Sacred Word:* _____

"Blessed are the peacemakers, for they will be called children of God."
—Matthew 5:9

Fourth Week of Advent: Centered in Peace

Date: _____   *Location:* _____   *Sacred Word:* _____

The fruit of the Spirit is love, joy, peace, patience, kindness, generosity, faithfulness, gentleness, and self-control. . . . If we live by the Spirit, let us also be guided by the Spirit.
—Galatians 5:22-23, 25

Fourth Week of Advent: Centered in Peace

Date: _____ *Location:* _____ *Sacred Word:* _____

"Peace I leave with you; my peace I give to you."
—John 14:27

CENTERED IN CHRIST

Forrest finally slowed down and let the candle light his path as he walked up the driveway to his sister's house. A peace settled upon him, and he felt uncharacteristically grateful for the time alone. Even though he was late, he almost wanted to linger a little longer in the quiet woods before stepping into the busy family gathering. As he neared his sister's house, he saw that people were gathered on the porch. He could hear their laughter and conversation. When his sister caught sight of him, she rushed down the stairs to greet him.

"Who is this stranger walking through the woods by candlelight?" his sister teased.

"I'm sorry to be late," Forrest apologized, "but I'm just glad to be here at all!" He briefly explained the flat tire and his need to use her Christmas gift to light his way through the woods.

"Well," she said, "you came at the perfect time as far as I am concerned. We just finished decorating our luminaries with the kids, and we came out on the porch to light them. We were all chuckling because we realized that no one had brought any matches to light the candles. At that moment, you inexplicably emerged out of the darkness, bringing the flame we needed to light our luminaries."

An unexpected tear slid down Forrest's cheek as he realized that he was exactly where he needed to be at just the right moment. Forrest and his sister joined the others on the porch, and he lit their luminaries from his single flame. Surrounded by the gentle glow of candlelight, even the youngest child stood still in the wonder of it all. Softly, Forrest's sister began to sing, and everyone joined her: "Silent night, holy night, all is calm, all is bright."

Forrest looked up to the sky, gratitude filling his heart in a way he hadn't experienced in a long time. In a clearing between the clouds, he noticed a single star shining brightly in the night sky. He took a deep breath, looked around him at those he loved, and whispered, "Thank you, God, for slowing me down and letting a candle light my way."

Jesus is born! The Light of the world has arrived, and the darkness cannot overcome it. Over the past four weeks, we have slowed down and let the candles of the Advent wreath light our way to Christmas Day. We have colored mandalas, lit candles, and prayed regularly to center ourselves in God's gracious presence. We have savored the season and tried to resist the temptation to rush through it. And, now, we have arrived at Christmas.

The culmination of the weekly candle-lighting comes on Christmas Eve when we gather to light the Christ candle at the center of the Advent wreath. For many, the Christmas Eve candlelight service is a deeply cherished tradition of our collective church life. Standing in the sanctuary aglow with candlelight is a precious moment seemingly suspended in time when hope for the coming year feels almost tangible. All our candles—burning with light—are lit from that single Christ candle at the center of the Advent wreath. As we pass the flame from one candle to the next, each light is not diminished. Instead, our collective light grows brighter as it is shared. Slowly and with great care, we pass the flame from one to another until everyone present has been touched by the light of Christ. We then raise our candles and voices together as we sing the beloved hymn about the silent and holy night when the Christ child was born.

> Our collective light grows brighter as it is shared.

Jesus, Emmanuel, God-with-us, Holy One, Wonderful Counselor, the Prince of Peace is born! By any name, we welcome the greatest gift of all: God's presence with us. From the moment of Creation, God's image has been embedded in each and every human being. Even so, God realized that we needed a more tangible way of understanding what it means to live into the fullness of God's image within us. We needed a Light among us to follow. God sent Jesus to light our path, to show us what it means to live fully, and to encourage us to love God, ourselves, and one another.

God's immense love for us is a mystery almost beyond comprehension. But the birth, life, death, and resurrection of Jesus make that mystery far more understandable because we share the same journey. Jesus walked, talked, ate, laughed, wept, and slept just like us. The tangible humanity of Jesus helps us understand the mysteries of faith that are beyond words.

> The Spirit helps us in our weakness; for we do not know how to pray as we ought, but that very Spirit intercedes with sighs too deep for words.
>
> —Romans 8:26

We can imagine what it may have been like on the night of Jesus' birth. We can smell the hay in the manger and the animals gathered around; we can see the shimmering star in the sky; we can hear a baby's cry in the night. We become a part of the miracle of the nativity through our imagination and our senses.

In much the same way, using our senses while we pray helps us engage with the mysteries of faith that are hard to otherwise convey. Tangible methods of prayer help us express our sighs that are too deep for words and create a space for their release. This Advent, we have embraced the spiritual practice of coloring mandalas as a tangible way to pray and lift our sighs and deepest longings to God. Coloring and prayer have united our hands, our heads, and our hearts as we draw closer to God's presence at the center of our lives. We have colored our way to Christmas, and the visual prayer journal we have created is a Christmas gift to ourselves. We can look back at these prayer mandalas and remember our journey through Advent. If the act of coloring and praying has become a meaningful spiritual practice, may we consider how to continue contemplative coloring beyond the season of Advent.

Christmas is here! God is with us! May we never lose sight of our God who will be with us today, tomorrow, and every day. Christmas invites us to welcome the Light of the world into the manger of our hearts. May we have eyes to

See the light. Be the light. Share the light.

see God's light shining around us. May we embody the light of God shining from within us. And may we center ourselves in hope, love, joy, and peace so that we may share this light with others. Throughout the year to come, may the simple blessings of Christmas inspire us to color and pray, letting the Light of the world illuminate our way.

CANDLE-LIGHTING LITURGY
FOR CHRISTMAS DAY

Prayer of Invitation

Jesus, Emmanuel, Prince of Peace, as I light this Christ candle and remember your birth, help me slow down and turn my attention to you. Shine your light into the places of darkness in my life. Illuminate me with your presence so that I may share the gifts of hope, love, joy, and peace with the world. You have come to bring hope to the hopeless, love to the lonely, joy to the brokenhearted, and peace to the troubled. May I have eyes to see this Christmas miracle in all that I do. Amen.

Lighting the Advent Wreath

Light all four candles of the Advent wreath and the Christ candle.

Scripture Reading

John 1:1-5

In the beginning was the Word, and the Word was with God, and the Word was God. He was in the beginning with God. All things came into being through him, and without him not one thing came into being. What has come into being in him was life, and the life was the light of all people. The light shines in the darkness, and the darkness did not overcome it.

Music

"Silent Night, Holy Night" (United Methodist Hymnal #239)
(Look up the hymn listed above, and sing or read the fourth verse aloud.)

Silent Coloring and Prayer

Choose a length of time for sacred silence and coloring that is best for you or for your group. The Christmas Day mandala can be colored however you choose as you celebrate the Light of the world that has been born this day.

- Begin your time of silence with these words: "God, help me to be still and centered in you during this time of contemplative coloring."

- End your time of silence with these words: "Lord, hear my prayer. Amen."

Questions for Contemplation and Conversation

- Where do you see the light of the Christ child in the world around you?

- How can you embody that light in your daily life?

- How can you share that light with others?

- How will you continue to grow your contemplative process, either through praying with mandalas or other spiritual practices?

Closing Prayer

Gracious God, light my path so that I can move forward with the gift of Christmas in my heart. Open my eyes to the light of the Christ child born each day in the manger of my heart. Fill me with an awareness of your presence in all that I do, all that I say, and all that I am. Encircle me with your light. Whisper to me in the silence. Take my inward contemplations and guide me to outward actions, led by the light of Christ. Slow me down. Open my eyes. Fill my heart. Hallelujah! Amen.

Christmas Day: Centered in Christ

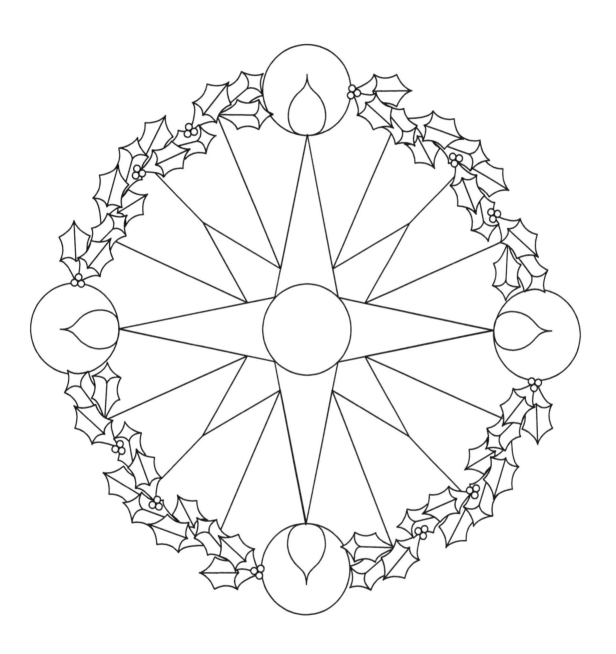

CPSIA information can be obtained
at www.ICGtesting.com
Printed in the USA
LVHW03s1018121018
593324LV00001B/1/P